Albert Camus

Albert Camus

By Robert de Luppé

translated from the French by
John Cumming and J. Hargreaves

Funk & Wagnalls / New York

Library of Congress Catalog Card Number: 68-22177

First American edition published in 1968

Funk & Wagnalls,
A Division of Reader's Digest Books, Inc.

Printed in the United States of America

CONTENTS

IT WAS thought necessary to include an account of Camus' third novel, *La Chute (The Fall)*, in this English edition: I am responsible for this and for the extension of the bibliography to cover some English translations and certain critical articles not listed by M. de Luppé. The English versions of the quotations from Camus' works were made by the present translators. The English titles of the collections of essays by Camus, *Noces* and *L'Envers et l'endroit*, are those used by Mr Philip Thody in his translation of the *Carnets*.

The following abbreviations have been used: MS for *Le Mythe de Sisyphe*, and HR for *L'Homme Révolté*. Page references are to the original French editions published by Gallimard of Paris.

JOHN CUMMING

London, 1965

MY INTENTION in this essay was to retrace the development of Albert Camus' ideas, starting from a privileged moment of insight, which "on a street-corner or in a restaurant's revolving door" eclipses everyday settings and opens our hearts to the poetry of the world, and arriving eventually at the controlled thought of *L'Homme Révolté (The Rebel)*, the schematic form of *La Peste (The Plague)*, and the restrained anguish of *Les Justes (The Just)*.

Since then, Camus has become even more exact in his thought, in his analysis and in his style. The landscapes in *L'Exil et le Royaume (The Exile and the Kingdom)* are more realistic than even the "hill-top" of Tipasa he had recalled so warmly only a short time before; the conscience of the *juge-pénitent* in *La Chute (The Fall)* is more complex than the charitable soul of Rieux; the mists and gold of Amsterdam are conveyed more precisely than any previous setting . . .

The path lengthens and the initial ardour is spent; now the traveller is nostalgic for the place from which he started; he looks back to measure the distance that he has come; he even retraces his steps to return to the original source of his inspiration. In *L'Été (Summer)* he wrote with affection of Tipasa, his youth and his love of the world. In his preface to the new edition of *L'Envers et l'endroit (Betwixt and Between)* he makes no apology for the simple and deeply-felt images that inspired him, but speaks of the "unique spring" or "central point" from which he would never wish to be separated . . . He would like to banish the temporal distance which affects the written work, and "begin anew" like Meursault in *L'Étranger* *(The Outsider)* : "I feel a vague conviction that if I do not manage to rewrite *Betwixt and Between* one day, in spite of so many efforts to forge a language and renew myths, I shall have accomplished nothing."

Let us try once more, with Camus, to understand that initial inspiration which nourishes his work.

Paris, December 1958

THE ACCIDENTAL death of Albert Camus in January 1960 appears to set a final seal on his work at the very moment when it seemed possible to see a desire for renewal through a "return to the initial sources of inspiration". The year 1960, so Camus confided to Giacomo Antonini (See the special number of the *Nouvelle Revue Française*), was to be devoted to a major novel, *Le Premier Homme (The First Man)* : "I have drawn up an outline and set to work in earnest. It will be a long task. But I shall finish it." If this sketch ever sees the light of day, we shall be able to continue our affectionate discourse and take up again the broken thread of Camus' life and thought.

Whatever the fate of his unpublished works may be, the shocked reaction to the news of his harsh death is a sure confirmation of the position his other writings have won him.

Paris, May 1960

ALBERT CAMUS was born on 7th November 1913 at Mondovi (Province of Constantine) in Algeria, where his family were agricultural workers. His father, who was killed at the front in 1914, was French, while his mother was of Spanish origin. He studied at Algiers University under difficult conditions: he was in turn a salesman of car accessories, a meteorologist, a clerk in a firm of ship-brokers and at the Préfecture. He was also an enthusiastic sportsman. After becoming a *Licencié ès Lettres* in philosophy he was awarded the *diplôme d'études supérieures*, a higher degree, for a dissertation on St Augustine and Plotinus. Sickness prevented him from sitting for his *agrégation*.

His passionate interest in the theatre was already evident: he founded the Théâtre du Travail and then L'Equipe and both produced and acted in plays. He staged a work entitled *Révolte dans les Asturies (The Revolt in the Asturias)* and written in collaboration with his friends, which depicts the rebellion of the Oviedo miners in Spain, in 1934. He adapted André Malraux's *Le Temps du Mépris (A Time of Contempt)*, André Gide's *Le retour de l'enfant prodigue (The Return of the Prodigal)* and the *Prometheus* of Aeschylus; he staged Charles Vildrac's *Paquebot "Tenacity" (The Steamship "Tenacity")*, Ben Jonson's *The Silent Woman*, Jacques Copeau's adaptation of *The Brothers Karamazov* (in which he took the part of Ivan), and Pushkin's *Don Juan*.

He travelled more or less haphazardly, visiting Spain, Italy and Czechoslovakia—countries which appear in his early works: the collections of essays *L'Envers et l'endroit (Betwixt and Between)* (1937) and *Noces (Nuptials)* (1938).

He worked as a journalist in Algiers, and then in Paris, and joined the Resistance. When the Liberation came he was appointed editor of *Combat*; he relinquished this post in 1947 and his editorials were published in 1950 as *Actuelles*.

He had already made a name for himself in the literary world. On the advice of Malraux, Gallimard had published *The Outsider* (1942) and *Le Mythe de Sisyphe (The Myth of Sisyphus)* (1943). With the Liberation two of his plays became stage successes: *Le Malentendu (Cross Purpose)* and *Caligula*, performed in 1944 and 1945 respectively. *L'État de Siège (State of Siege)* and *Les Justes (The Just)* followed (1948 and 1950). In 1946 Camus visited the United States. In the following year he published *The Plague*, a work which marked him out as one of the masters of the post-war generation of writers.

His historical and philosophical examination of rebellion, *L'Homme Révolté (The Rebel)*, was published in October 1951 and his novel *La Chute (The Fall)* in 1956. Albert Camus was awarded the Nobel Prize for Literature in 1957: his speech of acceptance at the official dinner and his address to the students of Upsala University were published as *Discours de Suède* in 1958.

Camus spoke out in defence of the insurgents of East Berlin and Budapest, and demanded a reconciliatory policy in Algeria.

He was forty-six when he died in a car crash on 4th January 1960.

Some Influences

Camus has been influenced by André Gide's classicism *(romanticisme dompté)*, by the Russian novelists, Tolstoy and Dostoevsky, by Melville, the master of the absurd and author of *Moby Dick*, and by Kafka (although Camus states that he is not at ease 'with the fantastic').

But the place of honour should be given to the least known of his masters, Jean Grenier, who was his philosophy teacher and Upper Sixth Form master in Algiers. In January 1959,

Camus described at length the "revelation" granted him in 1933 when he read *Les Iles* : "I think that I already wanted to write when I read *Les Iles*; but I really decided to become a writer only after reading this book. Other books played a part in this decision. But then I forgot them. This book, on the other hand, has always remained alive for me although it is now twenty years since I read it." (Preface to the new edition of *Les Iles*).

Gide was a source of encouragement for what he already knew he had within him : Jean Grenier opened his mind to anxiety and doubt, and to a feeling for mystery and the sacred.

1. Camus' Thought

Basic Ideas

The Myth of Sisyphus (1943) and *The Rebel* (1951) contain the essential thought of Camus. Their central and connecting ideas can be clearly distinguished. At the same time, the ten years or so which separate the two books enable us to recognize the *movement* of thought as it develops in contact with life, for, as Camus himself writes, "thought is indissolubly joined to and moulds itself upon the experience of life".

A distinction must be made between the ideas expressed in *The Myth of Sisyphus* and those in *The Rebel*. Camus invites us to do this when he warns us in his preface that the description of an "intellectual malady" is not a definitive statement of his ideas, for *The Myth* is provisional: "one must not prejudge too hastily the position that is taken".

I shall try to link this work with *The Rebel*. Here again, Camus invites us to do precisely this, when—cutting across time—he attempts to join the two divisions of his quest.

THE MYTH OF SISYPHUS

Suicide

Camus opens the book on this theme; it is given pride of place since it serves to express the author's own beliefs. This

1

work is not, then, a *study* of suicide, but the exposition of an *attitude to it.*

Suicide poses the problem of the *meaning* of life. Beyond superficial motives—sociological or sentimental—it is the vision, often purely instinctive, of the *ridiculous* nature of life, which we support through force of habit: "To take one's own life implies that one has recognized, even if instinctively, the absurd nature of everyday habit, the absence of any deep reason for living, the senseless nature of daily activity and the pointlessness of suffering". (MS p. 15 et seq.).

But Camus rejects suicide. Life has no meaning, yet we must go on living: this contradiction leads to Camus' own answer and already emphasizes his *heroism.*

The Absurd

Camus describes with precision and detail the meaninglessness of life, which is experienced through the *emotions* and the *intellect.*

The sensation of the absurd: A feeling which is at the origin of thought and action, a *definite* emotion, although *confused* and *indeterminate, present* yet *distant.* (MS p. 24 et seq.).

Its birth: The sensation is unforeseen; you are seized by this sudden feeling "at the corner of the street or in a restaurant's revolving doors"; it is sudden and wretched precisely because nothing ordains it, because the emotion arises under the most banal, everyday circumstances; yet it changes everything. This experience is personal and impossible to communicate.

Its content: Camus lays particular emphasis on an awareness of the mechanical aspects of life, which is emotional in nature. A few unusually precise and evocative lines forcefully convey something that the individual *sees* and *feels* personally: "Getting up in the morning, tram, four hours in the office or factory, meal, tram, four hours of work, meal, sleep—Monday, Tuesday, Wednesday, Thursday, Friday and Saturday, always the same monotony: it's easy to take this path most of the time".

The automatic nature of our gestures corresponds to the

external rhythm of everyday life; the absurdity is not only outside us but within us, for men have something inhuman within
them : "There is an inhuman side to men, too. At certain lucid
hours, the mechanical aspect of their gestures, this pantomime
without meaning makes everything about them appear senseless. A man speaks into the telephone behind a glass panel; you
can't hear him but you can see his meaningless gestures, and
you ask why he is alive." Life carries on *easily* until the day
when the chance feeling of absurdity leads to uneasiness.

A vision of time: Not as a helper but as our worst enemy;
time is no longer a favourable setting for our plans, our
ambitions and the growth of our souls. To flaunt one's youth,
for instance, is ridiculous; by doing so, we emphasize the curve
of life which culminates in death : "during each day of an
insignificant life, time bears us along. But there always comes
a moment when we must come to terms with time. We live with
the future in mind : 'tomorrow', 'later on', 'when you have a
job', 'you will understand when you're older'. These incon-
sistencies are extraordinary, for, after all, the affair depends on
death. But a day comes when a man notices or says that he is
thirty. He affirms his youth. But at the same time, he places
himself with respect to time. He takes his place in its scheme.
He admits that he is at a certain point on a line that he must
follow all the way. He belongs to time and, from the horror
that takes hold of him, he recognizes time as his worst enemy.
Tomorrow, he was ardent for tomorrow, whilst his whole being
should have fought against it. This rebellion of the flesh is the
absurd."

The vision of the alien nature of the world: If nature is
familiar to us, the reason is that we trace on its surface the
plans of our habits; it seems familiar because we are in contact
not with nature but with the ideas or the desires that we project
on to nature. Contact with nature itself reveals something materi-
ally different from human consciousness. The world appears
dense and *alien* to us : "One degree lower and the world is
strange to us : we realize that the world is 'dense' and see to
what extent a stone is alien and indomitable to us; we reach an

understanding of the intensity with which nature or a landscape can rebut us. All beauty is basically inhuman, and these
hills, the softness of the sky, these trees in silhouette, as soon as
they lose the illusory meaning which we had given them, are
ever after more distant from us than a lost paradise. The primi-
tive hostility of the world wells up towards us across countless
years. For a second we fail any longer to understand it, since
for centuries we have found in it only the images and shapes
that we had allowed it beforehand, because from now on we
lack the power to use that trick. The world escapes us because
it becomes itself again. These stage sets masked by familiarity
become again what they really are. They move away from
us . . . One thing is left : that denseness and foreignness of the
world is the absurd."

Finally, and above all, a vision of death: Here there is no
contact—for we can have no experience of death—but an
absolute certainty. We shall die : therefore nothing has any
meaning and our human adventure is useless : "Finally I come
to death and to our feelings about it. Everything has been said
about this and it is only right to avoid the pathetic. Yet it is a
cause for boundless astonishment that everyone lives as if he
did not *know*. For in reality there can be no experience of death.
In fact, one can only experience what one has lived through
and been conscious of. In this respect, it is hardly possible to
speak of the experience of other persons' deaths. That is a poor
substitute—a mental exercise which is never quite satisfactory.
So melancholy a convention cannot persuade. Horror actually
stems from the mathematical aspect of the event. If time makes
us afraid, it does so because it gives us a demonstration the solution to which comes later. All eloquent dissertations on the soul
will receive abundant proof of the contrary, at least for a time.
The soul has disappeared from this inert body which no blow
can any longer affect. This elementary and definitive side of the
adventure is the feeling of the absurd. In the mortal light of this
fate, its senselessness is made apparent. No ethic and no effort
can be given any *a priori* justification in the face of the harsh
certainties that order the human condition."

The rôle of the intellect: Camus goes on, although rather artificially, to consider the *irrational* elements in the world, i.e. everything which is outside the principles of human reason. All he does here is to resume old philosophical arguments without many original contributions : the impossibility of distinguishing the true from the false, the impossibility of understanding (i.e. of establishing a coherent system), the failure of scientific knowledge and of self-knowledge. In short, the world resists the demands of reason; our reason cannot explain the world. Camus bases his argument on certain existentialist philosophies (those of Jaspers, Heidegger, Kierkegaard and Husserl) to which he refers in this section of the book.

Consciousness: Faced with an incomprehensible world and this derisory everyday life, and confronted by this pantomime which only death can end, consciousness comes into its own. Rather, consciousness, in a sudden confrontation at a street-corner, is the source of this new awareness. In this sudden confrontation the nature of the consciousness both declares itself and seeks a separate existence. The exact stages in this development shown in *The Myth* should be noted : (pp. 26-27).

Everyday life—hitherto simple and natural—becomes wearisome and sickening, because the identification of the mind with the automatic rhythm is broken;

Astonishment appears : how have I who am consciousness been able to identify myself with something which has no part in my nature ? Consciousness becomes separate and independent; it begins its own course.

Weariness, paradoxically, is *good,* because it has a "sickening" effect; indeed, it is because it is "sickened" that consciousness makes a spontaneous attempt at separation.

Consciousness, once discovered, is felt to be good—the only good and the real good, for everything begins in consciousness and without it nothing has any value.

It is this *moral consciousness* that Camus defends with increasing vigour in and through his works.

The definition of the absurd: This concept summarises experience for Camus, since it takes into account *the whole con-*

tent of experience : on the one hand the mechanical world, the *object* of awareness; on the other the *consciousness*, which has entered into awareness, and which—by this very act—escapes what it sees.

In the *broad* sense the absurd is everything which is without meaning : therefore the world is absurd (*The Walls of the Absurd* is the title of one of the Chapters of *The Myth of Sisyphus*) just as I myself am absurd.

In the strict sense of the word, the absurd is neither the world nor myself, but the *link* between the world and myself. This link is based on confrontation : the opposition of my consciousness to the *walls* which hem it in. The absurd is implied in the very shock of conscious discovery that desires are meaningless; it is the shock itself which consists of a sudden separation : "The absurd is basically a divorcement. It is in neither one nor the other of the two. It is born from their confrontation." (MS p. 48).

The world, therefore, is not absurd but merely *irrational*; what is absurd is the confrontation of consciousness, this desperate desire for clarity, with the irrational : "The irrational, human nostalgia, and the absurd that arises from their confrontation : these are the three characters of the drama". (MS p. 45).

Rebellion

What is the *reaction* to this experience? The *correct* reaction will be one which takes into account *all* the elements of experience, i.e. consciousness on the one hand, the irrational on the other.

First answer: suicide. This was referred to at the beginning of the book and enabled the problem to be demonstrated. But it is no solution to the question. Admittedly, it is a *logical* answer : if life has no meaning, I shall kill myself. But it does not accord with *experience*, because it evades one of the principal aspects : consciousness. The absurd is born of consciousness and must live as a truth; existential logic (or *absurd* logic) demands the continuance of consciousness.

Therefore the problem is reversed : "Before it was a question of knowing if life had to have a meaning in order to be lived. Now it appears—on the contrary—that it will be all the more worth living, the less meaning it has." (MS p. 76).

We must contrast with the suicide the person condemned to death : his death is a reality; he is to die in a moment; but he rejects this death at the very moment in which he is forced to be conscious of it. The one accepts, the other refuses; the one looks forward to, the other rejects death at the very moment when he is faced with it : "The opposite of the suicide, in fact, is the man condemned to death". (MS p. 78).

Second answer: hope. Confronted by the *walls of the absurd*, the consciousness seeks a new life and rests in the promise of a world which is the key to this world : the answer of hope is the affirmation that one day everything will be explained, that from this very moment onwards everything has a reason—even the irrational itself. Thus Camus defines religious faith and the metaphysics of consolation. He finds hope in precisely those writers who, like Kierkegaard and Chestov, *immediately* decided upon a separation of consciousness when in contact with the irrational aspect of the world. (MS p. 40 et seq.).

But, hope—like suicide—is not the honest answer to the premisses of experience. It is not consciousness which fades away, but the absurd which it has perceived; the consciousness remains, but its movement of hope makes suddenly transparent the walls that it could not penetrate; the irrational becomes assimilable and disappears. Consciousness, now deprived of an object, fades away in turn to slip once more into the repose of everyday life. Hope joins suicide in a common obscurity.

The true answer: rebellion. Faced with suicide and hope, two aspects of experience must be strongly affirmed. Firstly, consciousness, which must be retained as the most precious, clear and true reality, the only reality which is close to us in a world which is completely alien : "This senseless reason is what alienates me from the whole creation. I cannot negate it with a mere stroke of the pen. I must therefore maintain what I think to be true. I must support what seems to be so obvious, or even against me." (MS p. 74). Secondly, the irrational must be maintained; it is coupled with awareness in a tense struggle. It must be maintained not for its own sake—for man hates it—but because it is indispensable to the conscious life. For this reason, according to Camus, the heroic solution is to chose awareness and not repose, for we can remain truly awake only if we pay the price of this bitter vision of an incomprehensible world and a useless fate.

How can this experience be maintained? What is the answer? It is *rebellion*. Only rebellion sustains the two aspects and ensures that they are confronted: "It is a perpetual confrontation of man and his own insignificance. It is a demand for an impossible clarity. It throws doubt on the world at every single moment." (MS p. 77). Revolt is directed *towards the absurd*: it is a contemplation of the absurd; it projects the consciousness towards it: "To live is to endow the absurd with life. To do this is above all to contemplate the absurd. Unlike Eurydice, the absurd is lost only when we turn our eyes away from it." (MS p. 76).

Thus in *The Myth of Sisyphus* Camus defines the essential characteristics of his revolt. Rebellion is *courageous*; it is *lucid* since it is a clear vision of an object (the irrational);[1] it is *solitary*, since experience (met with quite by chance *at a street corner*) is rare and intensely personal—it involves nothing outside itself. It is a glorification of pride: "The spectacle of human pride is unequalled" (MS p. 78)—the pride of being at grips with a more powerful reality which is crushing and which at the same time can be resisted; pride in bearing defiantly the burden of life. It should, however, be pointed out that already in *The Myth* Camus lays more emphasis on the deeper aspects of human consciousness—the desire for life and for clarity—than on pride. Pride is only an auxiliary force, a means of sustaining the terrible task of keeping consciousness separate from the stupidity of everyday life. This rebellion is not a revolt initiated by pride, but a rising of conscience—the most truly human form of consciousness. Finally, revolt, although it triumphs over

[1] . . . or rather it sees clearly that the world is incomprehensible.

the world, is *without hope*,[2] since it springs from an awareness of death as an absolute end. Rebellion cannot endow consciousness with immortality.

Freedom

The vision of the absurd arouses consciousness and separates it from the sequence of everyday gestures; and yet we are encompassed by everyday life: we must go on living from day to day since rebellion does not permit suicide. Consciousness in revolt takes its place in the world: the road now opens on to everyday life. Camus asks what significance life can have in a world of this kind.

Life has a new meaning, for there is now no question of a return to repose: there is a definitive awakening—or, at least, the promise of such an awakening. Consciousness is armed with new weapons when it returns to the world.

It possesses the weapon of *freedom*: Camus contrasts the former slavery with this new freedom. The experience of the absurd has allowed a transition from the one to the other.

Before the experience of the absurd: the illusion of freedom—quite common to all—was accompanied by a real bondage to principles, prejudices, aims, functions: "Before encountering the absurd, man lives his daily life with aims, a concern for the future or finding justification . . . He works out his chances, he counts on 'later on', retiring or the work of his children." (MS p. 80). If we give our life meaning, we erect barriers and set ourselves firmly in the mould of a career or worries: "Thus I could act only as the head of a family (or the engineer, or the leader of nations, or the minor post-office clerk) that I am preparing to become". I have not chosen my career freely, since society, and its prejudices, influenced my decision.

After the experience of the absurd: all these aims disappear; all these principles are lost; they no longer have any meaning.

[2] Camus emphasizes the absence of any affective meaning from this idea; the absence of hope does not necessarily mean despair. He implies a lucid vision which is capable of producing happiness: "I must admit that this conflict implies a complete absence of hope (which has nothing to do with despair) . . ." (MS p. 49).

They once had an absolute meaning: I clung to them because I believed that they were absolute. Now, in the face of death, they fade into absolute insignificance. This awareness of death separates me from the aims with which I identified myself: "But after the absurd, all is disturbed. The idea that *I am*, the way in which I behave as if everything had a meaning (even if, sometimes, I said that nothing had)—all this is quite suddenly negated by the absurdity of a possible death." (MS p. 80). I am free because I am mortal: "The absurd helps me with this point: there is no 'afterwards'. From now on, this is the reason for my deep personal freedom." (MS p. 82).

Passion

When I am made free in this way, my behaviour in relation to the world will no longer be that of an automaton but will change. My conduct will have the following features:

The enjoyment of the immediate present: Before, *the everyday man*, confined by his projects, lived for an abstract future: his life was a dream. Ideas and aims are no more, and the absurd hero discovers the concrete present, enjoys the richness of the world and becomes a sportsman or a poet: he abandons ideas and replaces them with sensations.

The enjoyment of a succession of moments: The search for a series of moments begins with this discovery of the present moment. The world has so many faces: so many moments are allowed me until the moment in which I die. I must not lose a single one of them! I must extend the range of my experience as widely as possible: "The present moment and the succession of present moments before a constantly conscious soul—the absurd ideal". (MS p. 88).

The abandonment of distinctions: My freedom allows me a multitude of possibilities. Now that I have abandoned all principles, I am also free of personal choice; I shall neither make distinctions between possibilities, nor shall I refuse any of them: "Everything is permitted". And the absurd hero takes up the cry of Ivan Karamazov.

Quantity replaces quality: "Therefore we must live to the

full", exclaims Camus. "We must not dwell on a single impression, like Proust lingering over the scent of a rose : we must burst out on the surface of the world in a continual blossoming of sensations. We must not elaborate a single sensation, but experience them all; we must not allow ourselves the privilege of a single experience, but accumulate as many as possible." (MS p. 86). In short, "a belief in the absurd is equal to replacing the quality of experiences with the quantity". (MS p. 84). The success of an absurd life is marked not by depth but by simple duration, measured very prosaically in years : "Therefore, no depth, emotion, passion or sacrifice could make a conscious life of forty years and a lucidity extended over sixty years . . . equal for the absurd man . . ." (MS p. 87).

Bitterness: "Everything is permitted !" is a cry not of joy but of bitterness, for this boundless freedom comes from the experience of the absurd : it therefore implies an enduring awareness of death and is bound up with an indifference which isolates the soul.

Therefore the experience of the absurd, far from throwing me *outside* life, throws me *into* life by virtue of the terrifying awareness it has brought me. And it is a new life : the mechanical nature of everyday activity is rejected by our consciousness and replaced by the enjoyment of sensations. I have the courage to return to my work and to everyday life, because something has changed in the relationship between my consciousness and the world.

But Camus is very careful to point out that there is no question of a joyous life over which no shadows fall. Since this new life is the result of an experience of the absurd, it implies constant awareness of death; only this awareness makes life possible, and only by means of it can the new life be entered. The experience of the absurd sends us back to life, but our new lucidity implies a certain burden : the enjoyment of varied sensations is not hedonism, for it requires courage and effort.[3]

[3] Camus provides three models: Don Juan, the actor, and the conqueror (or adventurer). They are realizations of living in the absurd : "I am choosing solely men who aim only to expend themselves or whom I see to be expending themselves". (MS p. 96).

We have examined the ideas which are central to Camus' outlook: suicide, the absurd, rebellion, freedom and, finally, passion. We have been able to follow, stage by stage, the path which leads from a moment of awareness to the gamut of sensations. At the outset there is the single print of the individual consciousness: at the end, there is absolute dispersion. Quality has been replaced by quantity.

However, Camus is not unfaithful to his early experience in *The Myth of Sisyphus*. He does not want moral consciousness to be immersed in the life of the senses. He does not forget that consciousness is the only thing that matters; although aroused, quite by chance, on a street corner, it must remain watchful. Although he advocates an endless succession of sensations, at the same time he demands the continual and underlying presence of consciousness, which alone lends intensity to sensations. We all have the same share of experience but we are not all *aware,* therefore these experiences are more often than not stillborn. From this new viewpoint, while remaining faithful to Camus' intention, we can assert that *quantity depends on quality*. Quantity does not deny quality but on the contrary stems from it; for if consciousness is not present at any given moment, the moment is not enjoyed, and we fall back into the monotony of everyday life. Camus advocates faith in the present as, "a succession of present moments", but he emphasizes that it can be so only for a mind which is always conscious; and that we can live sixty years rather than forty by all means, but we must make sure that our whole life is controlled by awareness.

Finally, the emphasis on quantitative experience again elevates consciousness. If we remove the hierarchy of values we endow consciousness alone with value: no doubt this is how we are meant to interpret the following statement in *The Myth*: "Where lucidity reigns, the scale of values becomes useless". (MS p. 87).

Is there a basic contradiction in *The Myth*? Between the moment of awareness and the expenditure of sensations: between quality and quantity? The answer is in the negative, for there is a continuity of thought in the service of the quality of consciousness discovered in the experience of the absurd. If we read *The Rebel* in this light, we shall find continuity between *The Myth of Sisyphus* and the later work, and at the same time the undivided nature of Camus' thought will be made clear.

THE REBEL

This book is intended to be an *historical* analysis of rebellion; it is not, like *The Myth*, a doctrinal description. History, however, is a stumbling-block to a process of thought clearly outlined in the first and last pages; history is set in a framework of principles which, to a certain extent at least, attempt to escape from history. For this reason, *The Rebel* is a development of the thought contained in *The Myth*. An examination of a few new ideas (murder, creative revolt, excess, the ideal of moderation) which are central to the book will suffice.

Murder

The Rebel appears at first to be a series of reflections on murder: the question "Should I kill myself?" posed in *The Myth* is followed here by a new question: "Should I kill other men?" The fact that Camus has chosen murder as the starting point for his exposition shows:

His concern with the present: He wishes to affirm his position when confronted by, and against, the world as it is; or rather, he wishes to define a system of *conduct*, for contact with the present leads to practical rather than theoretical problems. Camus' attempt to understand this "is an attempt to understand my own times" (HR p. 13)—and we live in an age of murder, when murderers are judges and the innocent are the accused.

Camus feels an intellectual need for *contradiction*. We have already observed this in *The Myth*, when discussing the notion of suicide. First premiss: life has no meaning; second premiss: I must not, however, take my own life. Thus *conscience* is pre-eminent. And now: first premiss: everything is permitted;

second premiss: I am not allowed to kill a human being.
The dignity of the conscience common to all men is again made
apparent.

A change of orientation: Murder implies a *second person*,
therefore humanity as a whole is involved.

Creative Rebellion

We must follow the path dictated by consciousness. The transition from *The Myth* to *The Rebel* must be emphasized; it is
a transition made clear in the importance given to the idea of
rebellion—to the detriment of the notion of the absurd—and in
the change of emphasis within this notion of rebellion.

The transition from the absurd to rebellion

The Myth of Sisyphus takes the form of a description of the
absurd, i.e. of everything which rends the consciousness and
opposes its aspirations. It is a useful description, for it is through
this voluntary "rending" that the consciousness assumes its
separate existence and is preserved.

The Rebel: The experience of the absurd is certainly necessary, because it makes a clean sweep of prejudices and ready-
made principles, and frees consciousness from its chains by
supplying the weapon of *doubt*.

But we must pass beyond the experience of the absurd : "It
is impossible to see in this sensitivity and in the nihilism on
which it is based anything other than a starting-point". To
remain on the level of the sensitivity and the nihilism on which
the absurd is based is the error of our age : "It has been the
mistake of an entire epoch to state, or to take as received (on
the basis of a desperate emotion) general rules of action the
evolution of which, considered as emotion, was to overstep its
bounds". (HR p. 21).

The experience of the absurd contains two contradictory
elements : the consciousness which demands clarity, and the
world deprived of meaning. The confrontation of these two
aspects demands a creative act which can overcome the contradiction : "After which", Camus writes, "the glass and its

fixed reactions must be shattered, so that one may take the ineluctable way of the absurd—the way by which its very bounds may be overstepped". (HR p. 21).

The following essential affirmations should be remembered :

—the absurd, taken separately, does not give rise to any rule of action;
—it is valid only as a starting point;
—it is in fact only an auxiliary, because it is contradictory : it sets two conditions which must be overcome by a creative act.

This ineluctable process through which the absurd is overcome, is the rebellion which sets the two elements of experience against one another. The experience of the absurd bears direct witness to one thing : my rebellion.

A change of emphasis within the rebellion

The notion of rebellion is central to *The Rebel*; it has appeared already in *The Myth*, but now it is enriched with fresh analyses.

The Myth of Sisyphus: Emphasizes the irrational element, since consciousness is awakened, and remains awakened, as a result of this contact; rebellion is useful to consciousness inasmuch as it is opposed to consciousness.

The Rebel: Emphasizes consciousness and the *desire for clarity,* as opposed to obscurity. This desire is fed by rebellion. Rebellion is useful in that it is positive. Camus extends this idea : in *The Myth* consciousness is awakened and *then* rebels; in *The Rebel* revolt bursts out and arouses the conscience as it does so : "Consciousness is born of rebellion". (HR p. 27).

Of course, rebellion does not *create* consciousness, for the value precedes the action. Camus takes good care to point out that he *is not an existentialist,* that is to say : for him, essence precedes existence : "Why rebel if there is nothing lasting to preserve?" (HR p. 28).

Camus ends with a positive affirmation : "There is such a thing as human nature . . . contrary to what contemporary philosophers maintain". (HR p. 28). This is an allusion to Sartre, which he makes even clearer : "This value which exists before all action contradicts those purely historical philosophies which assert that value is attained (if it is ever attained) through action".

Even if action is not creative, in the true sense of the word, it is nevertheless the only way to *revelation*. Camus even uses the word *basis* : "I must point out, before going any further, that the basis of this value is rebellion itself". Camus describes how the refusal of oppressive power results in affirmation—man's accession to awareness of a previously unknown aspect of his nature which is now suddenly recognized as his most intimate and free possession : until he rebels man does not really feel this identification, i.e. "*I am my* free conscience".

Rebellion therefore brings values to light.

Description of the Conscience

Rebellion brings to light not a vague sense of values, but a conscience with definite elements—with a structure or, at least, aspirations to a definite structure.

Communion with others: Human *nature* is an environment in which every consciousness participates; to rebel is to accede to this environment : "The slave makes his stand for all men at once; in him there is something . . . which is a place common to all men . . . where they are all one; in rebellion, man is no longer alone, but one with all his human brothers . . . I rebel : therefore we are". (HR p. 36).

We are concerned, therefore, not with an egotistical movement but, in most cases, with a sacrifice. In *The Myth of Sisyphus*, on the other hand, the emphasis is placed on the solitude of the rebel, faced with the obscure world which he is alone in discovering and sustaining : hence the pride which, in Camus' later works, replaces services to others.

Friendship: This is a matter of the heart. We must distinguish between the *idea* of man and man as he actually is : rebellion demands that the affective part of man—which cannot be reduced to an idea and which can serve only existence—should be taken into account. Friendship was excluded from *The Myth* intentionally (Camus mentions it only once).

The desire for unity: It is essential that the conscience should aspire to unity. In unity reside *duration*, *clarity* and finally happiness; "happy unity", sighs the nostalgic mind. This unity would cure us of our condition, which is at once uncompleted by death and *dispersed* by evil; for it would assemble within itself all understanding; and evil, joined to unity, would no longer be the dark abyss it is. In the name of unity, Camus goes so far as to imprint a new element on his thought: "The suffering of a child is not repellent in itself, but the fact that there is no justification for this suffering is not justified . . . The revolt against evil remains, above all, a demand for unity." (HR p. 129).

The appeal for a life of diversity, for exhaustion in the experience of the largest possible number of sensations, is followed by a song in praise of unity—a serious and no longer triumphant song reminiscent of a religious hymn to the One: "Rebellion is an ascesis, though it is blind". It is blind because the conscience in revolt does not simply have to regain unity (since it has no previous existence) but create it, or rather not abandon a futile quest. It is futile because—and this is important—the mind's cry of longing for unity arises from a contradiction caused by the assumption of paradoxical terms: the conscious mind struggles in an irrational and dispersed world. Unity has no meaning, since the world is not a harmonious extension of the focal point of consciousness. When lucid, the mind knows that its desire is only a desire, and not participation in a unity which has already been achieved.

Therefore we can see Camus' formulations as a kind of development in hesitation, leading from the religious to the negation of the religious; from hope in God to a refusal of this hope; from aspiration to unity to the realization of absolute dispersion: the rebel "seeks, without realizing it, a moral or a religious truth. Rebellion is an ascesis, though it is blind. If the rebel blasphemes, then, it is because he hopes to find a new God. He is shaken by the first and deepest of religious experiences, but, in this case, it is a religious disenchantment." (HR p. 129).

In the transition from *The Myth of Sisyphus* to *The Rebel*, the consciousness is enriched by essential determinations which set it in final contrast to the world and link it to other minds. Just as the experience of the absurd has aroused it from sleep, rebellion has nourished it and given material for growth. This is a growth made possible by strength, according to Camus' forceful definitions: "Rebellion ... breaks open one's being and allows it to overflow", or again, "The source of revolt is a principle of superabundant activity and energy". (HR p. 30).

In *The Myth of Sisyphus* and in *The Rebel* we find the same fidelity to the idea of the human mind and conscience, an idea that no other can replace. In *The Myth* this light within us is not put out by the triumphant affirmation of sensation : on the contrary, the two are linked. In *The Rebel* the intellectual glorification of revolt again pales before this light : "It is not rebellion in itself which is noble, but the aims it imposes on one". (HR p. 130).

This moral consciousness now realizes itself in action and— for Camus—in artistic creation.

2. Camus' Thought

Action

ONCE CONSCIOUSNESS is aroused, it demands action as a means to self-realization. There is no longer—as there was in *The Myth of Sisyphus*—any question of the sad necessity of a return to everyday monotony; external constraint is no longer exercised by a detestable automatism, for necessity is determined by the conscious mind itself.

Some action, then, must be taken; but what action is it to be? Can rebellion, as it has been defined here, determine conduct? "Can we find a rule of behaviour apart from religion and its absolute values? This is the question set by revolt." (HR p. 33).

The novelty of this question, in relation to those posed in *The Myth of Sisyphus*, should be noted. The experience of the absurd led to the blossoming of sensations; it did not dictate behaviour or lay down rules of conduct, since the values of action were abolished. "Live your life to the full" was the advice given in *The Rebel*, but the problem is how to find a structure, an order or *rule of conduct*.

In order to discover such a rule, Camus becomes a historian, or—more precisely—a *historian of his own time*. Valid action —real works—must be based on this confrontation with history, in opposition to all the deviations and reversals of the original impulse. Modern and contemporary history will be the privileged field of exploration, for it is cut from the coarse stuff of rebellion. History is removed from its *sacred pedestal*; by the same token, rebellion becomes the human dimension. The excesses of history will therefore be the excesses of rebellion. Here, according to Camus, the historian of our times will find the thread he needs to guide him. "To take rebellion as the 'explanatory principle', as the 'fundamental theme', is to explain in part the direction and almost entirely the excesses of our time." (HR p. 22).

In this search for just action, we shall need to detect unjust action, that is, all rebellion that does not remain faithful to its first principle: "By following its actions and observing its results, we shall have to say, every time, if it remains faithful to its initial nobility or if, on the other hand, through carelessness, or madness, it turns into a frenzy of tyranny or servitude" (HR p. 35).

THE BREACH OF FAITH

Our path leads us from the analytical study of revolt to the evidence of history:

The structure of rebellion: Camus resumes the analysis commenced in *The Myth of Sisyphus*. Rebellion is the confrontation of the lucid mind with the irrational world in which evil and suffering reign (it must be borne in mind that in *The Myth* the irrational and automatic aspects of the world are emphasized; in *The Rebel* weight is laid on suffering and murder); therefore rebellion is the tension between positive and negative. A breach of faith is the abandonment of one of the two conditions: it is a refusal of total responsibility.

This idea of resignation has already been discussed in *The Myth*, in the context of an entirely personal solution to the absurd, and not in relation to all action in the wider community of men. On the one hand, we have seen hope arising from the victory of lucidity; and, on the other, sucide as the consummation of the defeated conscience. In *The Rebel* we find that the same resignation, in this new perspective, gives rise to murder.

Absolute negation is rebellion when unfaithful to the positive value that it defends.

Absolute affirmation is rebellion when unfaithful to the underlying vision of the absurd; consciousness extends a positive answer to nature as a whole, and accepts evil.

Murder: This is the immediate consequence of the breach of faith. To kill is to forget the human community to which consciousness had acceded by virtue of rebellion. The conscience is denied in a position of absolute negation: I arrive at the statement "everything is permitted", and I kill another person. Suffering is forgotten in a position of absolute affirmation: I kill, and by killing I add to the sum of evil.

Therefore, unjust action is the transition from the relative to the absolute, from the limiting *tension* to the apotheosis of the only god; and, above all, from courage to weakness, from the struggle against nature to the inclination which leads us effortlessly to the very centre of evil.

But, before giving a precise definition of *just action*, we shall refer, with Camus, to the evidence of history.

THE EVIDENCE OF HISTORY

Camus distinguishes between the history of the idea of rebellion, and factual history; on the one hand we have literature and on the other, revolutions: metaphysical revolt is followed by historical revolt.

METAPHYSICAL REVOLT: This is the "means by which a man rises up against his own condition and the whole of creation. It is metaphysical because it questions the ultimate aims of man and of creation." (HR p. 39 et seq.). At the same time it defends a positive value which is rejected in absolute negation and affirmation.

Absolute negation: Camus selects the Marquis de Sade, the "dandies" of the romantic rebellion, and Dostoevsky for examination; after very detailed studies, he finds in all of them the same ignoble image of murder.

Absolute affirmation: Stirner and Nietzsche, although they take different paths, join the writers already referred to in the same acceptance of evil.

HISTORICAL REBELLION : This is the transition from thought to action. An idea is born of metaphysical revolt and an attempt is made to mould reality according to this idea; in this sense, rebellion considered historically attempts to become revolution : "The experience of rebellion is, initially, limited. It is only an incoherent act of witness. Revolution, on the other hand, starts with an idea. In fact, it is the insertion of concepts in to historical experience, whereas rebellion is only the movement which leads from individual experience to an idea." (HR p. 136 et seq.).

Here again, we meet with murder; no longer is it simply accepted or advocated—it is *practised*.

Regicide: Camus gives an explanation of the French Revolution. The Christian King, the representative of God on earth, is killed, and Reason is set as an absolute ruler in his place; but Saint-Just's proclamation of abstract and total virtue, through ignorance of the actual and limited condition of man, leads to the Terror.

Deicide: The absolute affirmation of the moralists of the French Reign of Terror is followed by the absolute negation of the Russian terrorists; the natural virtue of Rousseau is succeeded by the historical thought of Hegel. The absolute no longer reigns over history, for history itself is the absolute. Justice and truth are no longer present at the origin of action : instead they become the *results of action*. The actions themselves are of little importance, since these virtues will triumph in the end ! The means hardly matters if the end is reached ! We are again confronted with murder. Camus makes a distinction between :

—individual terrorism (i.e. that of the Russian nihilists, 1820-
    1905);
—State terrorism, either irrational (fascism) or rational
    (marxism).

There is progress in the transition from one type of terrorism to another : but it is progress in murder, from the exception to the rule, from the individual to the collective. Murder is the universal rule in modern times. Therefore, Camus centres *The Rebel* on the question: *"Is murder permissible?"* He does so by means of his concern with the present age, and as a reaction to the systems established before our very eyes.

Such systems are founded on a form of rebellion that places excessive emphasis on one of its constituent conditions. Paradoxically, the desire of the human conscience for unity is expressed in crime, on either the individual or the national plane. A human being or an entire nation is thrown into murder by a fanatical longing for unity. *The excess of the absolute*—to use Camus' expressive phrase—have introduced nothingness into the world; this is the return to slumber described in *The Myth of Sisyphus*, but in our time it has condemned thousands of men to death.

The desire for unity is inverted, since instead of lending new perspective to life, it destroys all life. It is an inverted love of one's fellow-men, for it is hatred of man extended until it becomes a hatred of all creation.

In the face of this criminal absolute, and in the face of hatred, the distinctive features of Camus' thought are made clear.

FIDELITY OR THE IDEAL OF MODERATION

The *just* action required (which is called *just* by virtue of its fidelity to rebellion) is the indissoluble union of moderation and love.

Moderation

Moderation is the recognition of limits in face of the excesses which culminate in murder; it is fidelity to the true principles of rebellion.

We must not be reluctant to return once again to the analysis of rebellion. Camus himself returns continually to this subject, as if returning to an initial spring from which strength and wisdom are drawn. Rebellion is a confrontation of the conscience and the obscurity of the world; in the terms of value used by Camus in *The Rebel*, it is *tension between good and evil*. This tension is not accidental but essential to these two notions; indeed, consciousness is only discovered in and through this vision of evil. In the same way, evil has come into the world only through conscious awareness; therefore good and evil are linked, because the one gives rise to the other. By the same token, they are not absolute but *relative*, being *limited* by each other. Evil is not absolute, since its existence depends on the consciousness that sustains it; good is not absolute, since it is discovered only when the conscious mind is confronted with evil. This observation of Camus is *experimental*: it is no more than a development of the peculiar experience described in *The Myth of Sisyphus*. The notions of *moderation* and *relativity* come to the fore. According to Camus, the action of rebellion gone wrong is that which, unfaithful to its origins (i.e. to actual experience), forgets the connexion between the conscience and its object. The person in revolt sets up one of the two terms as an absolute; simultaneously he destroys the other term. This perspective enables us adequately to consider all the characters in the historical drama related by Camus. Some, forgetting the reality of evil, lay claim to an uncompromising absolute and to a pure and total and therefore *inhuman* virtue that the facts will always belie.

If men kill in the name of abstractions, the massacre is bound to spread beyond all moderation, since no human being is capable of so pure a virtue as that demanded; we all deserve to die. Others abandon the pure element of rebellion—lucidity—and see the world as ruled by absolute evil alone; therefore everything is permitted, and they kill. Yet others think that good will come from evil: that one day, so to speak, evil will blossom out into good; while they await this joyous day, or in order to hasten its coming, they kill.

Therefore Camus rejects optimism and pessimism; or rather, these terms have no meaning for him. He is not a Rousseauian optimist, because he believes that evil is inherent in human nature. Of course, the human conscience has a certain power over evil; Camus demands the calling of a crusade to lessen the suffering and anguish of mankind. But even if we suppose everything possible to have been done, little children will still die. We can lessen the evil that we cause through our own fault; we can perfect nature, but essential evil remains: "Man can overcome everything in himself that should be overcome. He should put right everything in the world that can be put right. And when this is done, children will still die unjustly, even in the perfect society. The greatest proposition open to man can only lessen numerically the suffering in the world. But injustice and pain will continue and, no matter how limited they are, they will still offend." (HR p. 374). Camus recognizes that Dmitri Karamazov's "Why?" will never be silenced in historical time. In the lecture he gave to a group of French Dominicans he said: "As for myself, it is true to say that I feel a little like Augustine before his conversion, 'I looked for the source of evil: and there was no end to it'." And Camus adds: "But it is true that I also know, together with some other men, what has to be done".[1]

Evil, therefore, is an ineluctable reality; to believe that it can be abolished is in itself a temptation to use *totalitarian* means to achieve the triumph of *total* good; this is a return to evil. So Camus rejects optimism: "The echoes that we hear at the end of this long adventure of rebellion, are not calls to optimism, for which we can have no use in the extremity of our anguish". (HR p. 374).

The rebel who is faithful to the sources of his experience will not take up one of those extreme positions which, in the name of Rousseau and Hegel, have ravaged Europe throughout two centuries. The faithful rebel will be *aware of certain limits*. He will be lucid about the evil that surrounds him and is inherent in the universe against which his rebellion is directed. He will also be lucid about the inward evil inherent in his own condition as a human being: "If rebellion exists, it is because lies, injustice and violence are part of the condition of the rebel". (HR p. 352). This lucidity will lead to moderation by protecting

[1] *Actuelles I*, "The Unbeliever and Christians", p. 217.

the rebel from all illusion: the mortal illusion of the pharisee who, proclaiming that his virtues are irreproachable, will never-the less add, through his acts, to the injustice of the world. A claim that one is not an accomplice in murder or lies of any kind is a direct acceptance of murder and lies. The rebel "cannot, therefore, make an absolute claim not to kill or lie, without renouncing his rebellion and accepting, murder and evil, once and for all". . . . In short "He recognizes the good and yet, despite himself, does evil". (HR p. 353). Confrontation is the link that joins and brings life to good and to evil: if evil cannot be accepted, but on the contrary is rejected in horror, it is still necessary; or rather, it is the *perception* of evil that is necessary, as the sole condition for the consciousness to reach awareness and experience the qualities that determine it. For Camus, therefore, there is no question of being an optimist (i.e. of hoping that evil will be defeated) or a pessimist (i.e. one who expects evil to triumph), but rather of living on the level of the confrontation of good with evil. Here again we encounter the major concern of *The Myth of Sisyphus*: to live in the present and not in the future. The present is the continual struggle to sustain this vital consciousness. There is no question of comfort or of despair: the question is one of confrontation. The heroism involved in Camus' reaction to suicide reappears in his encounter with the problem of evil.

This encounter leads to the creation of a living ethic, which confronts the two deviations: on the one hand, *the absence of any ethic,* and, on the other, a *formal ethic.* In fact, Camus notes that a formal, immutable and abstract ethic leads to the same negation of the rights of the conscience, as do the proclamations of cynics, or nihilists. The true ethic of rebellion is *concrete* and active: it is part of daily life and part of the life of the individual and that of the nation as a whole. It is an ethic of the continual effort to maintain moderation or balance in all things and it is accompanied by the wearying intransigence that this implies.

Action in social life: At this point, Camus considers communal life and asks if there can be any use for action defined by moderation : "What is the political significance of such an attitude? And, above all, is it effective?" (HR p. 361).

Rebellion *requires action*. An initial question must be asked : is rebellion necessarily prolonged by action on the social plane, or does it on the other hand culminate in *abstention*? Since that form of rebellion which is unfaithful to its own origins is prolonged in violence, surely faithful rebellion would demand non-violence? I rebel; therefore I withdraw to the mountain and wash my hands of all concern . . . Camus observes that this is an attitude common to many modern poets. It would appear to be a justifiable attitude, for is not a withdrawal from the city of men in our time a means of purifying oneself of violence and hatred? Is it not a way of escape from a mechanical and degrading life? A natural incline would appear to lead from the philosophy of rebellion to the abdication of social and political responsibility.

Camus answers once more that this would be a betrayal of the origins of rebellion. Far from rejecting action within the city of men, rebellion requires such a course in order to reach fulfilment. Revolt is essentially a *mediating value* between two mutually exclusive realities : human consciousness and the world. It is a mediator because it leads to the confrontation of these two elements; it dethrones them as claimants to absolute importance and returns them to the state of mutual relativity. Non-violence is not the attitude proper to the rebel, but the attitude of a conscience that closes its eyes to the world, turns away and *consents*. Violence, on the other hand, arises when history is elevated to the status of an absolute value (Hegel) and the human conscience, which is outside history, is forgotten. Rebellion, however, confronts the conscience with history, in order to test and strengthen it in this encounter. Therefore the action of a just conscience in social life chooses neither the abandonment of social life nor the abandonment of true consciousness : it arises from rebellion. The *rebel* will act not from any sense of duty, nor because he is ambitious, but because he is faithful to his own rebellion : "What, then, can the rebel's attitude be? He cannot turn away from the world and from history without denying the very principle of his revolt; he cannot choose eternal life without resigning himself, in one sense, to evil." (HR p. 354).

Action is necessary for the rebel consciousness. Paradoxically, the *refusal* of history is coupled to the *acceptance* of history. This action will be *restricted*. Faced with the dilemma of a choice between violence and non-violence, the rebel will choose *limited violence* when he takes action; he will be a revolutionary, but only under certain *definite conditions* : violence for him "must . . . retain . . . its provisional character of a solitary criminal action and must, if it cannot be avoided, always be joined with personal responsibility and an immediate risk". (HR p. 360). For the rebel, should excessive injustice make violence unavoidable, will obey not a doctrine or reasons of state in the brief moment in which he inflicts violence, but the human values and institutions which are the living expression of such abstractions. Camus defines certain limits; in recommending moderation he is of our time and at grips with its realities.

The Rebel is closely linked with *Lettres à un ami allemand (Letters to a German Friend)*, written during the Occupation. Camus, as a member of the French Resistance, answers violence with violence; but he sees the difference between one violence and another : he divides honour from dishonour.

This action will be *effective*. It may even be the sole effective action. Even this qualification is unnecessary, since risk is an accepted factor. When the just action is the promotion of a movement for social reform, for example, the rebel will not accept the silencing of the voice of conscience in the name of expediency : he must not allow this voice to be stilled, even for a moment. A voice objects : "But the revolution will wither away ! A good end justifies the means !" Camus would answer : "I do not know if the end is in fact good; I simply know that it has not been attained. I do not wish to be unjust today, in order to achieve justice tomorrow." In short, the just cause is one where the means—rather than the end—is just; for the means is concerned with the present moment and therefore defines our existence. Expediency must not be confused with "efficiency"; the one brings into social life the values that radiate from the conscience; the other destroys all values in the name of future happiness. Camus reminds us "that there are two kinds of effective action : one is like the typhoon and the other like the sap in a plant". (HR p. 361).

The action of the rebel is opposed to the absolutism of history; the latter is effective though not efficient : ". . . it has seized and retained power. Once it has obtained this power, it destroys the sole creative reality. Intransigent and limited action, born of rebellion, maintains this reality and simply tries to extend it more and more." (HR p. 361). True efficaciousness is inseparable from risk; there can be no revolution without risks : "A revolution which is set apart from honour betrays its origins; and its origins are in the realm of honour". (HR p. 361).

A few actual examples: These are merely outlined in *The Rebel,* which is not a political tract. In any case, is it possible to have a "politics" of rebellion in the same way as, say, Marxist politics? Indeed, there can be *several possible policies* of rebellion. The circumstances, structures and accidents of evolution vary : there is no question of establishing absolute laws, but of adapting them to circumstances. The politics of rebellion can only be *relative,* i.e. adapted to suit the facts. In this respect, *Actuelles* gives us more information than *The Rebel.* In this work Camus collected the articles he wrote for *Combat* in the period directly following on the Liberation. Here we encounter the rebel—a journalist in the city of men—seeking moderation when confronted by the threatening face of excess. He must continually re-establish the balance between truths which are good and truths which are evil. He must demand effort and courage when faced with facile optimism and destructive pessimism. No general programme is to be found in these articles. Yet we are in 1944-45, a time when the reconstruction of the country on every level is imperative. But : 1. Camus was the editor of a newspaper, which is not suited to the exposition of a general programme; 2. Camus has no such programme. He simply considers day to day events and tries to establish due moderation.[2]

In short, rebellion defines an *attitude*, not a doctrine. Certainly, Camus is very close here to the ideas expressed by Emmanuel Mounier and the contributors to *L'Esprit*.

Camus left *Combat* in 1946. He appears to withdraw from the city of men. Has he betrayed his own rebellion? Does he intend to join forces with the "Yogi" whom he has condemned?[3] This accusation would be unjust. The real answer is as follows:

Camus withdraws from the political struggle (which, in any case, he has never pursued as do real politicians) when the moment comes to choose between the real values of the conscience, and falsehood. Even the best of people are confounded in political life when it becomes worse than everyday life. At this point, the only way to save one's conscience is to withdraw. This sense of disgust has left its mark on *Actuelles*: "The world in which I live disgusts me . . ."[4] This disgust becomes indignation, for society *at present* is not only riddled with lies and with vanity, but causes many men to despair: "It is precisely this that I cannot forgive in contemporary political society: that it should be a machine to make men despair . . ."[5]

Camus does not become a revolutionary after the break with contemporary political society. He had been a revolutionary during the German occupation, but he was a *rebel*, and not an opportunist or a doctrinal theorist. Today, however, an *honourable* revolt would appear to be impossible. Camus believes that by becoming a revolutionary one accepts the means which betray the end; in other words, such a move implies

[2] The few problems of an immediate social nature selected by Camus for treatment in *The Rebel* (trade unions, mechanization) are examined precisely from this viewpoint of moderation and commonsense. We must neither reject nor blindly accept our age; we must simply redress the balance.

[3] See the reference in *The Rebel* to Koestler's *The Yogi and the Commisar*.

[4] *Pourquoi l'Espagne?* in *Actuelles*.

[5] *Actuelles* p. 249.

alignment with a political party, and this means alignment with violence and injustice.

Camus does not entirely accept the outlook of the Yogi, for *individual* action goes hand in hand with public action in the city of men. He denounced violence right up to his death, whatever the quarter from which it came : he condemned the repression in Madagascar, and those in Budapest and in East Berlin. *Actuelles III* is inspired with a hatred of violence. Beyond the claims of the "ultras" and those of the F.L.N., he tries to define the conditions for a possible agreement between two races (he was immediately reproached for "not taking sides"). The statement already cited must be completed : "The world in which I live disgusts me", writes Camus, and he adds at once : "But I am one with all men who suffer". Rebellion is linked with love.

LOVE

The just action is moderation, but it is also love; love leads it to completion, for the way of love is straightforward and sure.

This love is a love of the *concrete*; thus it leads to things and to human beings in their very substance, in their flesh and in their individuality; it dissuades the rebel from abstract doctrines and guides him into houses near to other living men, in a direct contact of man with his fellow beings. It is the way of true rebellion : "if it wants a revolution, it wants it for life and not against it. That is why it relies basically on the most concrete realities : one's job, or a village, where the very being and living heart of things and of men are met with. Rebellion demands that politics submit to these truths." (p. 368).

This love is also love of the *present*. The theme of the present moment upon which such emphasis was laid in *The Myth of Sisyphus*, is now given a more profound application; it is no longer directed to sensation but to the human being. To help another man today rather than tomorrow, not to delude him with hope but to share in his life; this is the continual duty and work of the true rebel : "This senseless generosity is the generosity of rebellion, which gives the power of its love immediately and rejects injustice without delay. It is honourable in that it does not calculate and gives everything to life at the moment and to men who are living now. Only in this way can it be fully generous to the future. Real generosity towards the future consists in giving everything to the present." (p. 375).

This love is also a love of the *relative*. Love of the absolute, in fact, becomes hatred and leads to murder : a frightful reversal. To love one's fellow men, humble things, the world and, above all, the humiliated, is to entertain true love. Yet again, according to Camus, this just form of love is the fruit of rebellion, which abandons the absolute: "Then one realizes that rebellion cannot be without an unusual kind of love. Those who find neither peace in God nor rest in history (the two absolutes) are condemned themselves to live for those who, like themselves, cannot live : for the humble and persecuted." (p. 375).

LOVE AND REBELLION : We have now seen rebellion discovering and fostering love—on three occasions. But surely there is some contradiction here. Is not Camus mistaken? Can rebellion give rise to or, at the very least, favour human emotion? In short, is one not forced to choose between love and rebellion? The answer is that there is no necessity for such a choice *on the level described by Camus*.

A contradiction exists for someone who discerns an absolute in love, a participation in divine love, whilst rebellion denies or rejects God. But who can honestly claim that he is consciously sharing in divine love? Our love is so relative and so restricted, that rebellion can in no way diminish it. To make such an accusation against Camus, in this context, is to flaunt an abstraction completely outside human experience.

The rebellion conceived of by Camus is informed with a purity capable of protecting love. It should not be confused, in fact (and Camus emphasizes this), with the negative conception of *resentment defined* by Scheler;[6] it is not hatred; neither is it envy, nor a desire for possession. It is a struggle against hatred; it is the source of sacrifice and unselfishness. Rebellion can there-

[6] p. 30.

fore enter the service of love; or rather it can direct it towards those objects which are its only possible sources of nourishment.

JOY: When this path has been traversed and lucidity is finally achieved, a hymn is permissible. The midday angelus is heard not on the peaceful air but on the ravaged battle-fields of rebellion. It is midday—the "midpoint of time" which moves with the very movement of history. Now joy arises: it is the relief which rebellion brings, a much greater reward than that of pride. This joy is the knowledge of life and the knowledge of death; it is awareness of the glorious and limited nobility and mortality of the human condition; it is the human consciousness given lucid knowledge of its own nature: "Now the strange joy is born which helps one to live and to die". The joy of rebellion is strength, freedom, courage and the strait gate and narrow way: "At the moment of highest tension, a straight-moving arrow will be seen; nothing will turn it aside, yet its freedom will be liberty itself". The book closes with this assurance.

The central thought of Albert Camus

We shall leave the unceasing struggle of the conscience in order to compare *The Myth of Sisyphus* and *The Rebel*. Striking contradictions are apparent:

On the one hand we have the negation of values, and on the other the affirmation of values;

In the one case everything is permitted, in the other not everything is permitted;

Indifference is opposed to love, pride to moderation, dispersion to unity, and quantity to quality.

Must we require Camus to make a *choice*?

Camus would reply that there is *continuity* between the two books.

Admittedly, in his introductory note to *The Myth of Sisyphus*, he states: ". . . it may be said that there is something *provisional* in my commentary: one cannot prejudge the position it entails". But this "description, in the pure state, of an intellectual malady" is an indispensable *first stage*. In the first pages of *The Rebel*, Camus in fact identifies it as *method-*

ical doubt; *The Myth* examines values methodically, in Cartesian style : with the definite aim of seeking a *certain* value. It is not a question of the *same values* in this transition from negation to affirmation; the two parts of the study are linked inasmuch as the values depicted in the first are conventional because they ignore the inescapable experience of death, whereas those in the second part are living because they are won through experience.

One book *progresses* from the other : no contradiction is implied.

Nevertheless, it should be noted that there is an *excess of doubt* in *The Myth*. The faithful description of *an intellectual* malady cannot *coincide* with methodical doubt : it must extend beyond it. For it is value *as such* that is rejected by the absurd negation, which simultaneously bars the way to any further movement.

But one value is preserved from *The Myth* : conscience. We have already seen that this is a moral consciousness which never turns its own weapons upon itself, and which remains faithful to its own experience even in its most extreme negations. It destroys only in order to maintain its integrity.

The doubt expressed in *The Myth* is directed against all values, but not against their *origin*. For this reason, values recur and blossom out with greater strength and reality in *The Rebel*.[7]

Camus' unique contribution to thought is this animation of moral consciousness, the development of its essential qualities of truth, justice, love and joy, by means of a rebellion against suffering and evil.

---

[7] This is also the reason why the "intellectual malady" described in *The Myth* does not coincide with the "absolute negation" analysed in *The Rebel*.

3. Camus' Aesthetic

CAMUS' AESTHETIC forms a link between his philosophical essays and his prose fiction or plays. It is an aesthetic inspired by rebellion that ordains the nature of his creative work.

The most important texts for a consideration of his aesthetic doctrine are:

The Myth of Sisyphus, the chapter entitled *Absurd Creation*.
The Rebel, chapter IV : *Rebellion and Art*.

Actuelles I, the lecture given at the salle Pleyel on December 20th 1948, entitled : *The Witness of Liberty*.

The *Nobel Prize Speech* of 1957.

It is possible to distinguish three different aspects in these texts.

First aspect. Absurd Creation (The Myth of Sisyphus).[1]

The mission of art

Art is "absurd" when it conveys the experience of the absurd; it is a sudden vision, granted to the awakened consciousness, of a mechanical and meaningless universe. The intention of the work of art is the determination of this universe, so that consciousness may be kept free: "The work of art is the only chance of retaining consciousness and determining its course".

[1] MS p. 129 et seq.

The characteristics of the work of art

Since the work of art has this mission, the following characteristics are imposed upon it :

Sterility: the really absurd work is meaningless, inasmuch as it resolves no problem for the author : ". . . It is ridiculous to say that my life finds meaning in it". It offers no explanation for life; it is opaque, as are the walls of the absurd. The reader will encounter a meaningless, mechanical and ridiculous succession of facts or gestures.

The Image: the work of art should simply reproduce the absurd in repeating it and in *miming* it : "Art is the great mime". The image found in the work of art is a faithful re-creation of this absurd reality. Art is the superimposition of images on a *meaningless experience.* The absurd technique is the use of lucid reason to produce an exact description, whilst keeping this creative intelligence in the background. Reason is used strictly in the service of the irrational; this is the paradox of *absurd creation.*

Diversity: the work of art is a multiplication of instances of the monotonous routine of life; simultaneously, there is an absence of any unity. The work of art is not a depiction of character; it is a description of a meaningless disorder.

The stature of the artist

The artist creates not in order to realize a certain hope and to give meaning to life, but in order to mark out clearly that which is deprived of meaning. Therefore his work is *useless.* It demands *patience* and *lucidity, courage* and *clearsightedness.* Creative art calls for a "daily effort, self-control, an exact understanding of the limits of truth, moderation and strength". It liberates from lies about the world and oneself; it is, therefore, an *ascesis.*

The Outsider follows these rigorous standards laid down in *The Myth of Sisyphus*; therefore this work has a unique position in French literature.

Second aspect. Rebellion and Art (The Rebel).

Art is no longer an expression of the absurd; it is now a definition of rebellion. The inclusion of a new element in Camus' aesthetic marks the step forward from the position previously outlined in *The Myth of Sisyphus*.

The art of the rebel

Art should integrate the elements of rebellion:

1. The world or reality,
2. Consciousness.

It should express the *tension* that joins these two elements together: "The creation of a work of art is a demand for unity and a rejection of the world".

Those artists who have proved unable to create at the level of this tension are not genuine artists, for they have been satisfied with either total rejection or complete acceptance.

First case: the absolute denial of reality: "Reality is completely excluded". (p. 331). The so-called artist creates a *substitute universe* which has no connexion with the world in which we live. The result is the romantic novel, edifying literature, the pastoral and such works as *Paul et Virginie*.

Second case: absolute affirmation; reality is accepted completely. This is so-called *realist* art (although it is never met with in the pure state), the mere "photographic" reproduction of phenomena.

Genuine art is truly creative inasmuch as it rejects reality whilst at the same time illuminating *certain aspects of reality*.

In fact, genuine art does not reject nature but reconstructs its dispersed elements:

Music represents a transition from disorder to form, from sound to melody: "Melody allows form to sounds which of themselves have none . . . A peculiar arrangement of notes . . . draws from natural disorder a unity that satisfies both the mind and the heart." (HR p. 316 et seq.).

Sculpture is the stylization of movement; it seeks to imprison the passing rapture of the body.

Subject painting immobilizes an action which takes place in time and space; it gives immortality to a creature on his way towards death; it removes the human being from the human condition: "Long after his death, between light and shade, Rembrandt's philosopher still meditates on the same question".

By virtue of the selection he makes, the *landscape painter* assembles and unites disparate natural phenomena.

The Novel

The rectification of the world which the artist brings about in his search for unity, finds its most effective expression in the novel.

The rectification of the world: Camus takes as examples the character in the novel and the depiction of love.

A "character" is human life—a human life with its development given a final unity, its course traced from birth to death. The uncertainty of our everyday lives obscures the nature of this course. A nostalgia for unity is the creative impulse of the novelist: "To know the estuary, control the river's course, and comprehend life, at last, as destiny—these are their real aims". (HR p. 322).

Love is given coherence in the novel. In life it is dispersed, intermittent and cannot be retained. The possession of love and the inability to retain it form the conflict of the lover: "I only one living thing had a definite form in this world, it would be reconciled." (HR p. 324). The two pages of *The Rebel* which deal with love are among the most beautiful and the most typical of all Camus' works (pp. 322-323). The cry of anguish that the reader hears as he reads them, is a cry from the depths of the soul; it is a revelation of the most noble and profound longing. These pages contrast strongly in tone with the rest of this largely historical work—but it was a necessary effect. This cry had to be lifted above its setting, for—in its way—it is more important than novel, essay or poem.

Nevertheless, the novelist provides love with what is lacking in life: duration, fidelity and unity; he creates the universe "where passions are never distracted, where people are subject to obsessions and are always therefore one another". In addition, he gives love *existence* by allowing it a style and a form. What form would the love experienced by Madame de Lafayette have without her *Princesse de Clèves*? . . . "no one, not even she herself, would have known its form had she not given it the bare line of a faultless style".

The novel is a rectification of the world as it is; in fact, genuine art does not *manufacture* an entirely imaginary world, separate from our own. It is *my own* universe, and therefore *my* suffering or *my* love, which is given unity within the structure of the novel. The same world is in question. In order to create a truly living unity, art provides a tension between *acceptance* and *rejection* of reality.

Camus illustrates this idea by comparing the American novel (of the period 1930-1940) with the work of Marcel Proust:

The American novel has been unable to discover what is living and beautiful in the real world, in order to give it unity. Its derisory representation of humanity shows a total rejection of reality. In fact, it is dedicated to the description of the automatisms of everyday life and to the monotonous repetition of our conversation. Man is observed behind a pane of glass, and the man observed is no more than a puppet. In this kind of novel, we encounted the *degraded unity* of repetitions; it is not a living unity.

Marcel Proust rejects reality in order to *accede* to a higher unity. He rejects reality, and paradoxically, indivisibly, he upholds it. *Remembrance of Things Past* is succeeded by *Time Regained*; the *extra-temporal* memory is the universe—our universe—transfigured: Proust reunites "into a superior unity, the vanished memory and the present sensation, the twisted foot and the happy days of times past".[2]

In his own works, Albert Camus follows the path which leads

[2] The Proustian memory of *extra-temporal* essences is granted existence by virtue of *actual* sensations. When Proust stumbles on a cobblestone in the courtyard of the hôtel de Guermantes *(the twisted foot)*, the pure essence of Venice is released . . .

from the American novel to *Time Regained*: *The Outsider* is followed by *The Plague*.[3]

Style

Style expresses the *tension* between consciousness and reality. It is the equilibrium between *form* (reality) and *content* (consciousness); it is a *new form*; it is "the corrective process which the artist engages in with his style and by a redistribution of elements taken from reality". (HR p. 332). Therefore, the style of the rebellious work will not be that of the absurd work:

The absurd work *imitates* everyday life; therefore it uses a flat and monotonous style.

The rebellious work *reconstructs* reality; the protesting human voice is integrated into the style of the work: the results are a new density and a new solidity.

Camus' change of style was intentional. Progress in his aesthetic ideas coincides with the evolution of his art.

Third aspect. The artist in the city of men: the artist as the witness to liberty.

In his address at the salle Pleyel *(Actuelles)*, Camus opposes *art* and *ideology*, the *artist* and the *conqueror*. The genuine artist rejects the society of slaves; the very dignity of art demands opposition to a totalitarian world and challenges its assumptions. Living unity is opposed to abstract totality; individuality to levelling down; and *understanding* to hatred. Artists, in our time, are the sole defenders of humanity; they alone appear to be on the side of life, as opposed to death; they alone are prepared to bear witness to the living reality of men, as opposed to the law.

Artists are *witnesses to liberty*.

Camus resumes his personal witness to these ideas, with incomparable rigour and amplitude, in his address to the students of Upsala University (1957).

---

[3] I am not trying to seek any parallel between *Time Regained* and *The Plague*. I merely wish to emphasize the fact that Camus, starting with a description of the absurd, eventually arrives at essential realities which escape the absurd.

4. Camus as Novelist

The Outsider

The Outsider, which appeared shortly before *The Myth of Sisyphus*, is a parable in illustration of the philosophy of the absurd. It is not merely an example of simple narrative fiction: the reader must examine its immediate imagery carefully before he can understand its implications and discover the thought that sustains it.

On the surface, however, *The Outsider* appears to be only slightly unusual in comparison with the general run of novels: it has characters, a setting and a plot like any conventional fiction.

Meursault is an unimportant clerk in an Algiers office. His mediocre life is unrolled before our eyes. He attends his mother's funeral, sleeps with Marie, a typist, and strikes up an acquaintance with someone. Then the drama takes place: he kills an Arab and is tried and condemned to death . . .

The tale is a simple one, but the totality of the world's absurdity is enclosed within it. A division of the novel into three stages will help to reveal the themes it illustrates.

Everyday Life

The Myth of Sisyphus tells of the sudden discovery of the monotony of daily life: "Rising, tram, four hours in the office or the factory . . ." *The Outsider* is the depiction of this mechanical procedure: The following is a typical passage; it

41

describes one of Meursault's Sundays—the day after his mother's funeral: "Marie had gone before I awoke. She had told me that she had to go to see her aunt. I realized that it was Sunday; this annoyed me: I've never liked Sundays. So I turned my head back into the pillow to catch the smell of the salt from Marie's hair; I slept until ten. Then I smoked in bed until midday. I didn't want to eat at Céleste's café as I normally did, because they would ask me questions, and I don't like that. I cooked some eggs and ate them straight out of the pan, without bread as I'd run out of it, and I didn't want to go down to buy some.

"I didn't know what to do after lunch so I wandered round the flat. It was all right when Mother was still there. Now it was too big for me and I'd had to move the dining-room table into my bedroom. I didn't use any of the other rooms now: I just lived in there with the straw-bottomed chairs that were rather the worse for wear, the wardrobe with its speckled glass, the dressing-table and the brass bed. I left the rest of the place to look after itself. After a while, to have something to do, I picked up an old newspaper and read it. I cut out an advertisement for Kruschen salts and stuck it in an old scrap-book where I put things I find interesting in the papers. After that I washed my hands and, finally, went out on the balcony."

He watches the usual Sunday scene; the young men are on their way to the cinemas in the centre of the town: "When they had gone, the street gradually became empty. The films must have begun by now, I decided. The street was now deserted except for shopkeepers and cats. The sky was clear but not blinding above the fig-trees at the roadside. The tobacconist brought a chair out on to the pavement across the street; he sat astride it and rested his arms on the back. The trams that had been crammed full a short while before were now almost empty. In the little café, *Chez Pierrot*, next to the tobacconist's, the waiter was sweeping the sawdust from the deserted floor. There couldn't be any doubt that it was Sunday.

"I turned my chair round and sat astride it like the tobacconist; it was more comfortable like that. I smoked two cigarettes, went inside to get a piece of chocolate and came back to the window to eat it. The sky darkened not long after and seemed to promise a summer storm. But it gradually cleared. Nevertheless, the clouds had left in the street a feeling that rain was coming; this made it darker. I stayed there for some time, looking at the sky."

Night falls: "Then the street-lamps were suddenly on: they made the first stars that were visible in the sky seem pale. I could feel my eyes tiring from watching the pavements, the people moving along them, and the lights. The street-lamps here and there revealed the oily cobbles; at regular intervals the trams went by, their lights shining on glistening hair, a smile, or a silver bracelet. A little later, fewer trams passed and the blackness of the night was already visible above the trees and the lamps; the street emptied imperceptibly; the first cat slowly crossed the space deserted for yet another night. Then I thought I ought to have some dinner. My neck was rather painful: I had been leaning across the back of my chair too long. I went down to buy some bread and macaroni; I cooked and ate standing up. I thought I'd smoke another cigarette at the window, but I found the air a little too cold now. I closed the window, and on my way back across the room I caught sight of a corner of the table in the looking-glass: I could see my spirit-lamp on it with a few scraps of bread beside it. I realized I'd managed to see another Sunday through, that Mother was buried now, that I'd be at work again in a few hours, and that when all was said and done, nothing had changed."

The Myth of Sisyphus shows us consciousness *identified* with the succession of everyday gestures. Such is the consciousness of Meursault; it is passive, bored and fatigued ("it's all the same to me", is a phrase he uses often). The sensations are elemental: drinking, eating, sleeping and smoking. He is a man to whom love, remorse and joy are foreign. He is left unmoved by the most affecting of human situations: neither the death of his mother nor the love shown by Marie can rouse him from his torpor.

The central theme of the novel is the *meaninglessness* of

Meursault's existence. His life has no purpose and no impulsion :
it proceeds blindly and automatically. It consists of movements,
a sequence of half-thoughts and crude sensations.

The reader is offered no consolation : there is no escapism
in the book. A reading of *The Outsider* is an encounter with a
dirty and impenetrable wall—the image of the human condition. Perhaps this is a means of self-awakening, or release
from mere disgust. But this feeling of disgust should not be considered as anything other than *good*, for it jolts the consciousness into nausea and simultaneously liberates it. *The Outsider*
corresponds to the decisive moment of emancipation described
in *The Myth of Sisyphus*.

The Trial

The circumstances of the murder: This unimportant clerk,
an uncomplaining victim of circumstances, kills an Arab whom
he does not know, on the beach. His crime is no more than the
mechanical result of a series of accidental events (the meeting
with Raymond, the decision to go for a swim) and passively
felt sensations (the glare of the sun, a dazzlingly clear stream).
Meursault fires, and he is brought to judgement.

The judges: They are men of principle and are therefore
alive to the emptiness of this *outsider* for whom conventional
values are meaningless. Meursault has no *conception* of filial
love; this makes him culpable in their eyes.

The lawyer: He defends the accused man, but his attach-
ment to principles places him—in spite of himself—among the
prosecutors. He asks him an important question : "Did you
love your mother?" But his client has no ready answer for
him : "Of course I'd been quite attached to my mother, but
that didn't mean anything. All normal men had more or less
sometimes wanted those they loved to die. At this point, the
lawyer cut me short and looked very disturbed. He made me
promise not to say that during the hearing, or to the examining
magistrate. Just the same, I explained to him that I was made
so that my physical state often affected my feelings. I was very
tired and sleepy on the day I went to Mother's funeral."

Meursault states a hard truth : "I felt like telling him that I was like everyone else, just like everyone else".

The examining magistrate: He also finds this distasteful : "Without any warning, he suddenly asked me if I had loved my mother. 'Yes,' I said, 'like everyone else.' Strangely enough, the magistrate senses some threat to himself : 'Do you want my life to be meaningless ?' he exclaimed."

The prosecutor: In fact, all these men are defending—against Meursault—the meaning that they have given to their lives. They are not alone in this : the whole of society is with them. On the day of the trial an occasional silence or murmuring show that the public agree with the prosecutor's indignation. There is no point of contact between them and this *outsider*.

First of all the prosecutor tries to establish *premeditation*. Meursault states that he killed the Arab *because of the sun*. Everybody in the court laughs, because everybody imagines his life is governed by purpose. Meursault confronts them with the reality of everyday life : "I was always concerned with what would happen next, today or tomorrow".

But the prosecutor's main point is the prisoner's *lack of feeling* : "The prosecutor began to speak about my soul : he said that he had addressed himself at length to the question of my soul, and was persuaded that I had none, 'gentlemen of the jury'. He said that there was nothing of the sort there, that there was nothing human in me and that I had no access to any of the moral principles that assure men a compassionate heart."

The method of *The Outsider* is much more than the cinematic depiction of everyday life. It shows the conflict between the pharisee and the publican, between society—jealous of its traditional principles—and the *outsider* who does not obey the laws of the game. In fact, Meursault is not an ordinary man, for he is without prejudices and without lies; nor is he a *rebel*, for he has not discovered truly living values. He is the brute in man : the human creature stripped naked, in all his misery; Meursault is truth disclosed.

This is why he encounters hatred. The pharisees feel themselves threatened and hasten to accuse him, in self-defence. They feel the threat to be all the greater, because the sole reward of this miserable life is granted Meursault and human values are made apparent : Meursault displays no human feeling, yet he has faithful friends;[1] he does not know what love is, and yet a woman loves him;[2] he is an outsider in the world, and continually the world offers him its colours, familiar sounds and extenuating, noble rhythm.[3]

The pharisees realize that this true life lies beneath the surface; not only must they defend their principles : they must also reject living values. They prefer their arid principles, and the *security* they offer, to the ardour of the human heart if these supports are removed. They reject the adventure which leads man from *The Myth of Sisyphus* to *The Rebel*.

Meursault is condemned to death.

Prison

The Outsider is an *absurd work*, although "absurdity" is not pursued to its logical conclusion : Meursault's rebellion is his awakening from the heavy slumber of everyday existence.

He is in prison and three themes appear in succession :

Hope: This is the temptation of the weak when confronted with death; When he realizes that he has been caught up in the inevitable process which leads from the sentence to the guillotine, Meursault tries to escape his fate : "At the moment I'm only interested in evading this automatic procedure". Is he to jump over the wall, or to change the law? Of course, there is still time to appeal.

Rebellion: The last assault of the enemy forces is the visit of the prison chaplain, who recommends the consolations of religion. This is the final blow : amidst the succession of injuries, rebellion takes shape, bringing with it the sudden aware-

---

[1] The restaurant-owner, Céleste, testifies in the prisoner's favour; he is unable to express himself clearly, but he manages to convey his belief that Meursault possesses a human quality that makes him worthy of friendship.

[2] . . . the youthful and easy-going Marie, with whom he goes swimming.

[3] The intentionally monotonous tone of the narrative is constantly interrupted with short and contrasting descriptive passages.

ness of the terrifying truth made clear in *The Myth of Sisyphus*: "Death is there as the only reality". (MS p. 81). At this very moment, consciousness drops its chains: it realizes the ideal of *The Myth of Sisyphus* by rejecting death at the very moment when death is forced upon it: the absurd is "at the same time awareness and refusal of death. It is, at the extremity of the condemned man's last thought, the shoelace that—despite everything—he can see a few yards away, on the very edge of his giddy drop. The opposite of the suicide, in fact, is the man condemned to death." (MS p. 77). 正反

Meursault is *lucid*: he *sees* the absurdity of a world where men must die, and he rejects this absurdity. At the same time, he is able to judge his own life and to *justify* it: "It was as if I had always been waiting for this moment and for this dawn, when I should have my justification". In the light of death everything is made equal; everything is reduced to the same level when one asks then "What does it mean?" Meursault knows that he was innocent when his judges found him guilty: "Nothing, nothing at all was in the least important and I knew exactly why". The absurd man is *innocent*.

Affection for life: Consciousness is awakened; the world is made clear: both the world that is to come, and the world that is passed away: "I think I was asleep: for when I woke up, I saw the stars shining down on me. The sounds of the countryside reached me. I could smell the night, the earth and salt; and I was refreshed. Summer was asleep, and its miraculous peace entered into me and filled me like a tide." The world is made manifest within his cell, as if in answer to his readiness to relive everything.

In *The Outsider*, Meursault passes through the stages depicted in *The Myth of Sisyphus*. At first he is so influenced by the blind mechanical movement of everyday life, that (like all of us) his humanity is almost lost; now he has liberated himself, rejected the temptation of pointless hope and, in the presence of death, has instinctively chosen not suicide but rebellion. His reward is the richness of feeling and the miraculous experience of the present moment.

Camus' style is adapted to these different stages; it is not a uniform style, for it is exactly varied to suit the different impressions of everyday life and of the life of the senses. To be more precise, Camus' own remarks on aesthetics help us to distinguish three styles:

The absurd style: This is strictly controlled in order to "mime" the absurdity of life: short sentences, neatly balanced in order to chop up into separate moments the continuous monotony of time: Sartre, in his essay on *The Outsider* in *Situations, I,* definies this as the use of "the precise, clean period—the sentence enclosed within itself".

The rebellious style: This differs from the absurd style through the addition of a new harmonic element: the artistic consciousness *observing* the absurd reality. This leads to a *transformation* of reality, achieved in *The Outsider* by means of *irony,* a subtle weapon in the hands of Camus (as he stated himself in *Combat:* "I do not reject irony"[4]). The section of the novel dealing with the trial should be read for examples of the use of this style.

The poetic style: Camus has not classified this style in his critical writings. Perhaps, this is because it is a style which represents the essential Camus as a man among other men, with no message to convey. He walks through Algiers, experiencing, seeing and feeling . . . But Meursault finds this poetic gift troublesome when he controls himself to "mime" the boredom of everyday life: he sees things too often through a poet's eyes. It does not seem to be the indifferent Meursault, but the Camus of *Nuptials* who describes the games played while swimming with Marie Cardona, and the details of a walk by the sea: "We got down from the bus on the outskirts of Algiers. The beach is not far from the stop, but to get there you have to cross a stretch of ground, quite high up above the sea until it slopes down sharply to the sea-shore. It was covered with yellowish stones, and lilies which stood out pure white against the harsh blue of the sky . . . We strolled between the lines of little

[4] "Autocritique" in *Combat* for November 22nd 1944. See also *Actuelles,* p. 41.

villas with their green or white fences : some, with verandahs, among the tamarisks; others unadorned amidst the stones. Before we reached the edge of this shelf, the stillness of the sea could already be seen, and, further again, a huge head of land rested in the clear water."

How is Meursault, *before his rebellion*, able to open his indifferent heart to the softness of the evening? In the van which takes him from the court to the prison, he re-experiences for a short time "the smell and the colour of a summer's evening . . . the newspaper sellers' cries through the now tired air, the sound of the last birds in the square, the sandwich sellers shouting, the trams screaming at the steep turns up in the town and the gentle movement of the sky before the harbour is enveloped in darkness".

Camus is a poet unable to silence his poetry; whether by intention, or not, he is—to a certain extent—untrue to his aesthetic, since he obscures his intended image of the world's absurdity.

5. Camus as Novelist
The Plague

THE DEVELOPMENT in Camus' work between *The Outsider* (1942) and *The Plague* (1947) corresponds to that between *The Myth of Sisyphus* (1943) and *The Rebel* (1951); the second of the two novels is a preview of the second of the theoretical works.

One of the characters in *The Plague*, Tarrou, states the problem about which this "chronicle" is constructed : "In short," Tarrou said, in a matter of fact voice, "I want to find out how one becomes a saint". "But you don't believe in God." "Precisely. Is it possible to be a saint without God? That is the only real problem that faces me now." (*The Plague*, p. 279).

This paradox is examined with sincerity and with acuity in *The Plague* : it forms the basis of this analysis.

I. THE IDEAL OF SAINTLINESS

It is not realized in Oran before the plague strikes the town. The theme of mechanical everyday life with which *The Outsider* was concerned is found also in *The Plague*.

Oran, in 194 . . ., resembles Algiers : its citizens are the same ridiculous automatons—the slaves of everyday convention : "The commonplace nature of the town's appearance and life must be emphasized. But you can spend your days there with-

50

out difficulty—provided that you have formed a routine. And since routine is exactly what our town encourages, you can say that everything is for the best." Once it is caught in the trap, consciousness goes to sleep : "The town is without attraction, vegetation or soul; after a while, it just seems restful and eventually you go to sleep there". (p. 16). This deep slumber is disturbed by no lightning-flash : the heart is not charged with a sudden shock, at a street-corner : "There are towns and countries where, from time to time, people suspect the existence of something outside their everyday lives; though, in general, that doesn't make them change their ways. Oran, however, appears to be a town without conjecture." (p. 14). Its inhabitants are concerned only with transactions, commerce and making money.

Tarrou: This absurd life is observed by a man whose consciousness is awake : Tarrou has a lucid mind. He is the "convert" of the absurd and an *outsider* in the town. He walks the streets with *The Myth of Sisyphus* under his arm, noting the meaningless details in a journal, retaining his awareness : ". . . a very unusual chronicle which seems to have a deliberate bias towards the insignificant detail". (p. 35). He takes pleasure in describing the bronze lions in front of the Town Hall, the dirtiness of the trams, droll interludes (an old man leans over his balcony to spit at the cats "firmly and accurately").

Tarrou is the absurd hero who has not passed entirely beyond the life of sensation : "From the beginning of spring he had been seen on the beaches; he was often in the water, swimming with obvious delight. He was good-natured, always had a smile on his face, and seemed devoted to all the normal pleasures without being their slave." (p. 35). Later in the novel he says, "I have not ignored anything in life". We shall meet him in the very thick of the plague.

SUFFERING : The town is scourged by plague; the appearance of the town is altered as the puppets become men in the midst of suffering : the automatism of everyday life gives way to pain. This provides the novel with a texture more resilient and richer than that of *The Outsider*. Man is stripped of the masks of convention, and his body and soul are laid bare to the flail of the plague.

Human bodies are distorted and twisted by physical pain; human mouths vomit whilst the plague sores, hard as knots of wood, suddenly release the pus enclosed within them. Camus gives us a sober description of these horrors; his respect for the human body is evident. His approach is the very opposite of that of Sartre and his second-rate disciples. The style of *The Plague* is that of a writer who does not shirk the extremities of real life, and who is guided by a lucid and wary moral consciousness.[1]

Moral as well as physical anguish is met with. The citizens of the plague-ridden town were formerly all Meursaults, with souls encased in slumber. Oran is sealed off, pestilence strikes and husbands and wives, brothers and sisters, as well as lovers are subjected to the torture of separation. This affords the novelist new subject-matter : no longer the complexity and minute details of everyday life, but the nuances of mental suffering, its degrees, the imprisonment of the human heart in waiting and expectation, and the supreme anguish—the gradual extinction and death of love.[2]

Joseph Grand: He is a minor clerk at the Town Hall, and could be another Meursault. He does not stick advertisements in an album, but—rather pathetically—is always rewriting the first sentence of a novel that he will never finish. He is *insignificant* and, like the *outsider*, symbolic of the absurd life we lead : "At first sight, Joseph Grand was no more than the minor town hall clerk he appeared to be. He was tall and thin, and seemed lost in his clothes, for he used to pick out suits that were too big for him . . . If you noticed the way in which he walked—like a student from the seminary, keeping close to walls, slipping into doorways—if your nostrils caught the slight hint of basements and cigarette-smoke," and all the marks of insignificance, "you

---

[1] This is the *authentic* realism called for in *The Rebel*.

[2] As we have seen, the two pages of *The Rebel* concerned with the theme of transitory love are among the most moving Camus wrote.

would admit that you couldn't think of him otherwise than sitting at a desk, diligently revising the price-list for the municipal shower-baths". (p. 56).

But only "at first sight" : he is quite different from Meursault, for he is *human*. He is not a stranger among us, but our human brother. He has exactly those feelings that were foreign to Meursault, and which were pronounced worthless by the absurd vision of *The Myth*.

At the stage we have reached with *The Plague*, it is no longer a question of false emotions, of rooting out the tares in men's hearts, but of the "real life" described in *The Rebel*. We are no longer concerned with the variations of pride exhibited by the pharisees, but with the humble virtues of Joseph Grand : "In a certain sense, you would be right in saying that he led an exemplary life. He was one of those men, as rare in our town as they are anywhere else, who are never afraid of their good inclinations. He said little about himself, but what he did say was proof of kind acts and an affection that no one in our times dares admit to. He did not blush when he said that he loved his nephews and his sister . . . He admitted that the memory of his parents, who had died when he was still very young, moved him. He did not hide his special liking for a certain church-bell near his place, that used to ring at about five every evening, and which had a pleasant sound." (p. 59).

Grand's life, therefore, far from being described as a series of events without significance, from a mother's funeral to the murder of an Arab, *achieves the dignity of human fate*; it is given form and unity by the novelist. Grand's suffering is given an "ideal delineation", like the love of the princesse de Clèves; it is arrested, like Rembrandt's philosopher, in eternal life.

One day he tells Dr Rieux his story : "He was still quite young himself when he married a very young, and poor, girl from his neighbourhood. In fact, he had given up his studies and taken a job in order to marry her. Neither Jeanne nor he ever left their part of the town. He used to go to see her at her house. Jeanne's parents would sometimes tease her silent, awkward suitor. Her father was a railwayman. He always spent his leisure hours sitting in a corner near the window looking thoughtfully out onto the street, his great hands flat on his thighs as he watched what went on down there. Her mother was always busy with her housework, and Jeanne helped her. Jeanne was so small that Grand felt anxious if she crossed the street. The vehicles seemed out of all proportion. One day they were standing by a shop-window that was specially decked out for Christmas; Jeanne looked at the display in delight, then turned to him and said, 'Isn't it beautiful!' He squeezed her wrist. That was how their marriage was decided.

"The rest of the story, according to Grand, was very simple. It's like that for everyone : you get married; you love each other still, for a time; you work. You work so much that you forget to love. The head of Grand's office hadn't kept to his promises, so Jeanne had to work, too. Here, you needed a little imagination to understand what Grand was trying to say. Mainly because he was tired, he let himself go, was silent more often, and didn't make his young wife feel that she was loved. A man who works hard all the time, poverty, no future to look forward to, the silent evenings at the table : in a world like that there is no room for passion. Jeanne had probably suffered. Nevertheless she stayed with him : you can suffer a long time without knowing it. The years passed. Then, after a time, she left. Naturally she didn't go alone. 'I loved you very much, but now I'm tired . . . I'm not happy at having to go, but it's not necessary to be happy to make a fresh start.' That was what her letter amounted to.

"Joseph Grand had suffered in his turn. As Rieux pointed out, he could have begun all over again. But, you see, he no longer had any faith.

"In short, he still thought about her. He'd have liked to write her a letter justifying himself. 'But it's difficult,' he said. 'I've thought about it for a long time now. While we loved each other, we understood one another without saying a word. But you don't love all the time. A certain moment came when I should have found the words to keep her, but I couldn't.' Grand blew his nose in a kind of checked napkin. Then he wiped his moustache. Rieux watched him." (pp. 96-98).

Grand is not spared by the plague (though he does not die); Rieux meets him: "At midday, when it was freezing cold, Rieux got out of his car: he had seen Grand some distance from him, almost glued to a shop-window full of roughly carved wooden toys. Tears were flowing steadily down the old clerk's face. Rieux was deeply moved when he saw them, for he understood them, and felt the same tears in his own throat. He remembered how the unhappy man had become engaged, standing in front of a Christmas shop-window, with Jeanne turning round to say she was happy. From the depths of the hidden years, from the depths of his fond misery, Jeanne's clear young voice had come to him: that much was certain. Rieux knew what the old man was thinking at that moment, as he cried; and the same thoughts were in Rieux's mind: that without love this world was a dead world, and that there always comes a time when one grows weary of prisons, of work and of resignation; a time when one urgently longs for the face of some other person and the miraculous and tender affection of another heart.

"But the other had caught sight of him in the window-pane. He turned round and leaned on the window to watch Rieux as he came towards him; he had not stopped crying.

" 'Oh, Doctor! Oh, Doctor!' he gasped.

"Rieux nodded to show that he understood: he was unable to say anything to Grand. He was one with him in his distress and the pain in his own heart at that moment was the grievous anger a man feels at the suffering all men share.

" 'Yes, Grand,' he said, at last.

" 'I wish I had time to write her a letter. To let her know . . . so that she can be happy without feeling remorse . . .'

"Almost violently, Rieux pulled Grand forward. The old man allowed himself almost to be led along, and went on talking, stammering out his half-sentences.

" 'It's lasted too long. You want to let yourself go . . . it's a strain. Oh, Doctor! I look placid, I know . . . But I've always found it a tremendous effort just to be normal. Well, now it's too much . . .'

"He stopped. His whole body was trembling and his eyes were inflamed. Rieux took his hand. It seemed on fire.

" 'You'll have to go home.'

"But Grand broke free, ran a few paces, then stopped, threw out his arms and began to sway backwards and forwards. He turned round on himself and fell on the icy pavement : his face was soiled with tears, for he was still crying. Some passers-by watched from a distance; they had stopped abruptly and did not dare to approach. Rieux had to carry the old man." (pp. 286-287).

SYMPATHY : The passage that has just been quoted is evidence of the author's affection for his characters, and of the compassion of Rieux as he passes from one character to another. This love is a direct response to suffering and is the recognition of a common human condition. The future analysis of *The Rebel*[3] is essentially present in *The Plague*; indeed, *The Rebel* can be read as a theoretical commentary on the fictional world of *The Plague*. There is a difference, however : this sense of common participation in human suffering springs directly from the spectacle of pain, in the novel; whereas in the theoretical work it is born of rebellion. The more profound vision of truth would seem to be that expressed in *The Plague*. The *direct* awareness of suffering awakens the moral conscience more surely than does revolt. In the novel, in any case, rebellion occurs *with* and not *before* compassion.

Rambert: He is a journalist by profession and the plague has trapped him in Oran during an assignment; he is unable to rejoin the woman whom he loves, in Paris. He tries in vain to escape. At the very moment when he does have a chance of leaving the pestilence-stricken town, he decides to stay.

He is divided between two truths : personal *happiness* and the *lives of others*. He must choose between these two conflicting

---

[3] Already present in an embryonic form in 1945, i.e. two years before *The Plague*, in *La Remarque sur la Révolte* (in the collection *Existence*, published by Gallimard).

aspects of reality. He could not validly deny himself happiness—
for which man is made—but also he could not validly reject the
existence of other men and act as if he were alone.

Let us follow the dialogue that takes place between Rambert,
Tarrou and Dr Rieux, where the conflict is most urgently
defined.

Rambert describes to his friends the measures that he is taking
to try to leave the town;[4] he refers to his guiding value, his love
for an *individual* human being: "Now I know that man is
capable of great actions. But if he is not capable of a great
emotion, he does not interest me." Rieux's answer is an affirmation that a decision to fight the plague is not a choice of heroism
as opposed to love; it is a choice that implies love for *all* human
beings: "Man is not an idea, Rambert". But he commends the
journalist at the same time, and endorses the values that guide
him: "You are right, Rambert, absolutely right, and nothing
in the world would make me stop you doing what you intend
to do: it's just and it's good". He emphasizes this when Rambert says: " 'Perhaps I'm quite wrong to choose love.' Rieux
looked straight at him: 'No,' he said firmly, 'You're not
wrong'." Thus Camus states and *maintains* the two terms of
the conflict.

A little later, the dilemma recurs.[5] Rambert has at last discovered a means of escaping from Oran, but, in spite of this, he
decides to stay (he has been a member of one of the relief
squads for some time). Rieux forces him to consider the other
term: " 'What about *her*?' he said very quietly". Rambert's
reply shows that he has not abandoned his *own* truth: "Rambert said that he'd thought it over again and that he hadn't
changed his mind, but that if he left, he would feel ashamed.
He wouldn't be able to love the woman he'd left in Paris in the
same way". Rieux reproves him again: he "looked up and said
forcefully that that was ridiculous and that there was nothing
shameful in preferring happiness". Rambert's rejoinder under-

----

[4] pp. 182 et séq.
[5] pp. 229 et seq.

lines the other truth : " 'That's true,' said Rambert, 'but it can be shameful to be happy on one's own.' ' "

Tarrou, who has said nothing so far, enters the conversation : all three want to *resolve* the conflict : "Tarrou . . . said that if Rambert wanted to share in other men's misfortune, he'd have no time to himself for happiness. The choice had to be made." But Rambert *refuses to choose*; he feels that he has not made a choice between two truths, but has decided on maintaining both aspects of truth. He answers: "That's not it . . . I'd always thought I was an outsider in this town and that your affairs didn't concern me." He has stated the first truth; now he affirms the second: "But now that I have seen what I've seen, I know that I belong here, whether I want it or not. This affair concerns us all."

Rambert is sure that he has not made a choice : he turns round to face his companions and questions them : "Have you made a choice and renounced happiness? Have you?" They are unable to answer him immediately : "Only Rieux turned to him. He raised himself with difficulty from the car-seat : 'Forgive me, Rambert,' he said, 'I don't know the answer'." And he adds : "Nothing in the world can make it worth rejecting what you love. And yet I'm doing just that, without really knowing why."

"Without really knowing why"; some kind of force controls them and pushes them beyond the terms of the conflict; while paradoxically integrating those very terms, this power impels them towards suffering humanity so that they may help men and try to save them. Will they achieve happiness afterwards? Perhaps happiness is rather to be found *within* a more extensive world—the world of all men who suffer. But does individual human happiness, the destiny of each man, undergo any essential change?

A precise answer to this question would necessitate a falsification of the characters Camus has created.

All we can say is that a response to suffering is the sole means of attaining peace : "After a silence, the doctor asked if Tarrou had any idea of the way that must be taken to find peace. 'Yes,'

said Tarrou, 'compassion'."[6] The way of the saint is the way of
love.

II.   SANCTITY "WITHOUT GOD"

The perception of other people's suffering awakens love and,
at the same time, rebellion. It is for the sake of love that man
rejects or denies God. Love and rebellion are the two fruits of
suffering. There can be no sanctity *with God*.

Evil is a scandal: neither the emotions nor reason can
justify it. Admittedly, man can hardly be considered innocent;
he is constantly *adding* to the total anguish in the world. Nevertheless, even if we suppose that one day war and crime are no
more, and that science has lessened the sum of human slavery,
little children will continue to die. Children die, and God does
not exist: these are the ultimate complaints of the rebel.

Rieux, confronted with the corpse of the judge's small boy,
says: "But that boy, at least, was innocent. You know that as
well as I do!"

The child had been in agony, whilst Rieux, Tarrou and
Father Paneloux stood round his bed: "Just then the child's
body was again convulsed, as if something had torn at his
bowels, and he gave a shrill groan. He stayed contorted like this
for a few seconds that seemed unending, his body shaken and
trembling convulsively as if his frail bones were bending under
the violent wind of the plague and cracking beneath the
repeated blasts of fever. After this sudden and fierce storm he
relaxed a little; the fever seemed to recede and leave him, fetch-
ing his breath in gasps on a damp and tainted shore, already
sunk, it seemed, in the repose that is death.

"When the parching wave touched him for the third time
and lifted him a little, the child recoiled from it and shrank
towards the further end of the bed; terrified by the flames that
scorched his body, he shook his head desperately and threw
off his blanket. Great tears welled up from beneath his inflamed
eyelids and flowed down his ashen cheeks. When the paroxysm

[6] Tarrou has just told Rieux his life history. (p. 278).

was over, the exhausted child contracted his bony arms and legs from which the flesh had faded within two days: he lay there, as if crucified, in a grotesque attitude on the disordered bed.

"Tarrou bent down and wiped with his great hand the small face stained with tears and sweat." (p. 234 et seq.).

The child dies: "Castel had moved to the other side of the bed and said that life had gone. The child's lips were parted, but no sound could come from them now: his body was lying amidst the disarray of the blankets, suddenly diminished, the tears not yet gone from the cheeks."

Rebellion is the just reaction to this anguish: the sole and spontaneous answer to such horror: "But Rieux was already leaving, so quickly and with such a look on his face that Paneloux stretched out his arm to stop him, as he passed.

" 'Come now, doctor,' he said.

"With the same fierce, quick movement, Rieux turned to him and declared passionately:

" 'But that boy, at least, was innocent. You know that as well as I do!'

"Then he turned away and passed through the doorway in front of Paneloux. He went to the other end of the school yard, sat down on a bench beneath the meagre, grimy trees and wiped away the sweat that was already trickling down into his eyes. He wanted to shout out again—to release the fierce bonds that cramped his heart."

Paneloux joins him; rebellion is now directed against the God to whom Paneloux claims allegiance: " 'Why were you so angry with me?' said a voice behind him. 'I found the sight of that child just as insufferable.'

"Rieux turned to Paneloux:

" 'You're right,' he said. 'Forgive me. But fatigue brings on anger. There are times in this town when all I feel is disgust.'

" 'I understand,' murmured Paneloux. 'It's revolting because it is beyond our comprehension. But perhaps we should love what we can't understand.'

"Rieux sat up suddenly. He looked at Paneloux with all

the strength and passion he could summon up, and shook his head.

" 'No, Father,' he said. 'My conception of love is different. Until the moment of my death I shall refuse to love a creation where children are put to the rack'."

Father Paneloux: He is a talented preacher. In this plague-stricken town he represents hope in a future life. He gives two sermons in the cathedral of Oran : they chart the route from triumphant faith to faith in the midst of despair.

First sermon.[7] Paneloux describes the plague as a punishment sent from God and as an opportunity to return to God. Seen from this point of view, evil has a reason for existing : it is an integral part of a divine scheme. Father Paneloux brings reason to bear on the problem of suffering and gives it a meaning. It is no longer an offence; the proper attitude is one of submission, not of rebellion.

But Dr Rieux believes that if Paneloux allows suffering a purpose, it must be no more than an *abstraction*—an idea—to the priest : "Paneloux is a scholar. He hasn't seen many people die and that is why he speaks with such conviction. But even the most obscure country priest who gives his parishioners the last sacraments and who has heard a dying man gasp for breath thinks as I do. He would seek to relieve distress before trying to prove its excellence." The experience of suffering may be fruitful, but that is no justification for human anguish : " 'Nevertheless you're like Paneloux in thinking that the plague can be beneficial, that it opens people's eyes and makes them think!' The doctor shook his head impatiently. 'Every human sickness does that. It can give some people a certain moral grandeur. But when you see the misery and pain that the plague brings, you would have to be mad, blind or a coward to give in to it'." (p. 144 et seq.).

Second sermon. Paneloux has watched the child in its last agony : he *has seen* the effects of the plague, and his abstract assurance has vanished. The *concept* of evil can easily be fitted into a system, but not the reality itself. Paneloux's easy convic-

[7] p. 111.

tion has been affected by the impact of reality on his consciousness: he is forced into the other party. He adheres to the absolute irrationality of faith, even though he had once preached acceptance of a divine order in all things: he now preaches faith as the blind acceptance of a scandal that the intellect rejects: "This is the faith; cruel in the eyes of men, but decisive in the eyes of God, that we must grasp".[8] (p. 243 et seq.).

Soon after, Paneloux dies of plague after refusing all medical aid; he dies, almost despairing, clinging to a tenuous and defective faith. "He did not know how to rebel"—that is the judgement on Paneloux offered us in the novel: he did not know how to die with the moral equilibrium of a lucid conscience, poised securely between rejection and acceptance, between struggle and peace. He was unable to love.[9]

III. THE "TRUE PHYSICIAN"

In *The Plague*, the saint *without God* is also the *true physician*. There are two classes of human beings, explains Tarrou: the torturers or the victims fall into one category and those who are both at the same time, into the other (the *innocent murderers*): "Of course there must be a third category; that of the true physicians . . ." (p. 278).

The physician: Actions based on love are limited. This, a

[8] Paneloux's second sermon reflects the general character of the "existentialist" philosophies criticized by Camus in *The Myth of Sisyphus*. The blind and desperate faith of Paneloux is undoubtedly Camus' portrayal of what he takes to be the real Christian position. cf. "Three Interviews" in *Actuelles,* pp. 224-225: The journalist has suggested the following as a description of Christian faith: "In the face of such suffering (the death of a child) the Christian can do little more than make an act of faith . . . But the Christian's act of faith is a submission of reason to the most shameful injustice: it is an act of resignation and escapism . . ." Camus replies: "I should not make so immediate and precise a judgement on the matter. Would it be true to say that the faith of Saint Augustine or Pascal is *resignation*? The honest course is to judge a doctrine by its most exemplary adherents rather than by the lesser practitioners. Although these are matters to which I give little thought, I have the impression that faith is not so much a form of peace as a tragic experience."

[9] Compare Tarrou's death with that of Paneloux. (cf. p. 307 et seq.).

very important theme in *The Rebel*, is illustrated in the day-to-day work of Rieux. He is a physician of bodies and not a healer of souls; he is concerned with the present moment and with the actual fleshly condition of man : the particular suffering or wound before his eyes. To love man is to seek to heal him, and not to save his soul for a debatable future existence : this is the difference between Dr Rieux and Father Paneloux. Othon's son has just died; the priest joins Rieux as he sits on a bench in the school yard; "Paneloux sat down by Rieux. He was deeply moved it was clear. 'Yes,' he said, 'yes, you are also working for the salvation of mankind.' Rieux tried to smile. 'The salvation of mankind is too impressive a phrase for me. I don't try to go as far as that. Man's health concerns me; his health comes first'." (p. 240).

"I don't try to go as far as that" : love is humble since it is concerned with small and concrete tasks; Rieux is simply concerned with the honest pursuit of his profession : " 'But I must tell you one thing : heroism doesn't come into all this. It's a question of honesty. That's an idea that may make you laugh, but integrity is the only way of fighting the plague.'

" 'What is integrity?' Rambert asked in a serious voice.

" 'I don't know what it means for others. In my case, I think it means doing my job'." (pp. 183-184).

The *true* physician brings into his work the realities he has felt : man's anguish, the common nature of the human condition, a rejection of suffering and a decision to fight unceasingly for its diminishment. "Suddenly Rieux gave a short, friendly laugh : 'Tell me, Tarrou,' he said, 'what persuaded you to take a part in this?'

" 'I don't know. My rule of conduct, perhaps.'

" 'And what is that?'

" 'Understanding'." (p. 149).

Dr Rieux: He is the chronicler of the pestilence : we have already encountered him several times in this discussion of *The Plague*. He tries to put the ideal of the *true physician* into practice when faced with reality. He has gradually enriched his life by putting it to the service of a great truth: "When I took up this profession, I followed it in an absent-minded manner, to some extent, because I just wanted to be a doctor, because it was as good a career as any other . . . And then, I had to watch people die." From that point on, the practice of his profession —even without the impulsion of any more metaphysical rebellion—has become a struggle against death. His work has a new sense of direction and, at the same time, it has been extended. Rieux does not make his visits to the victims of the plague alone. His mission of healing is extended to Grand, whose suffering is only within the mind and heart, and to Cottard, the insecure and guilty man.

The expression "true physician" must be understood in a more essential sense. The example of Rieux is an invitation to do so, for he does not restrict himself to bodily healing. Tarrou demands a fuller understanding of compassion.

The story of Tarrou:[10] His father was a Deputy Director of Public Prosecutions; he heard his father in court, demanding that a *living* human being be guillotined. At the age of seventeen, he left his family to devote his life to fighting capital punishment.

His agitation takes a *political* direction, at first; because the society to which he belongs condemns men to death, he must seek to overthrow that society. He joins a political party that claims to seek the preservation of human dignity. But he discovers that the means demanded of him is opposed to this end : he condones murder (there are always good reasons . . .) in order to bring about the end of all murder! He thinks his motives pure and yet, subtly, he has been tainted. Tarrou abandons political agitation : "The others can be the ones to make history". He will undertake the cure of individual, solitary action. Tarrou organizes the voluntary squads in the plague-stricken town; he is a medical orderly and almost a physician.[11]

But an *inward* activity is the source of this public action in the city of men—in Oran. The plague is a flail that strikes the

---

[10] p. 269 et seq.
[11] *The Plague* demonstrates the transition from *public* to *individual* action insisted upon so strongly in *The Rebel*.

body; but there is a corresponding scourge within, that brings out on men's souls the sores of hatred, falsehood and pride: "I know without any doubt (yes, Rieux, I know all there is to know about life, as you can see) that every man carries the plague inside him; because no one, no one in the world is free from it."

The external medical battle against the plague is matched by the internal struggle against the pestilence of evil, carried on only at the cost of a sustained effort: "What's natural, is the microbe. The rest: health, integrity, purity, if you like, comes from the will—from an unceasing use of willpower . . . Those who want to rid themselves of the plague experience an extreme weariness from which nothing will free them, except death."

Purity, in short, is the best way of helping others. Only the untainted will not infect others: this is a high ideal, and Tarrou practises it: "I only know that one must do what one can to rid oneself of the plague . . . That is a course that can bring men comfort; even if they're not saved by it, at least it ensures that they're done as little harm as possible and even, sometimes, a little good."

The "true physician", therefore, is someone whose outward action (which is not restricted to medical care) is based on an integrity of spirit that has *triumphed* over evil. The definition implies that few men have realized this ideal: "It's a fact," says Tarrou, "that you don't meet many of them and it must be a difficult road to follow." Tarrou himself is only on the way to the ideal: he is not yet a true physician. He belongs to the second class of men—the "innocent murderers" who, in the words of *The Rebel*, "know what is good, and yet do evil."[12] Sanctity without God is the aim of some of the characters in *The Plague*; but it is no more than an aim.

---

[12] In *The Rebel*, Camus would seem to disallow the reality of the "third category". Perhaps he is too honest to describe an ideal outside his experience, and stops short at the "average" proper to man. Perhaps, too, he believes that the abstract nature of this ideal is *dangerous*: a belief that evil can be conquered in a human soul would too readily lead to the sectarian intransigence of Saint-Just.

6.[1] Camus as Novelist

The Fall

CAMUS' THIRD NOVEL, *La Chute (The Fall)*, was published in 1956. It was not originally planned as a novel, but as a short story like those published in 1957 in the collection *L'Exil et le Royaume (Exile and the Kingdom)*. Most of these stories were written before *The Fall*, of which Camus made at least five versions before the final one.

The Fall seems more bitter in mood than either *The Outsider* or *The Plague*; the themes of both these novels are restated in the later work, in a more aphoristic form.

The structure of Camus' last novel may be seen as a variation of the diary-form used in *The Plague*. It is a monologue in which the narrator addresses a casual acquaintance—or merely the reader and himself. The listener's presumed reactions are stated by the narrator in the course of his one-sided conversations. The sombre tone and moral irony of the book, its ambiguous effect, are similar to those of its literary ancestors, Melville's *Pierre; or, The Ambiguities* and Dostoevsky's *Notes from Underground*.

Clamence is a bachelor and a once-successful Parisian lawyer who specialized in "noble cases": "I am sure that you would have admired the precision of my tone, the niceness of my emotion, the persuasion, fervour and controlled indignation of

[1] cf. Translator's note, p. vi.

my defence". (*The Fall*, p. 24). He addresses a casual stranger in the sleazy Mexico City bar in Amsterdam where he now "practises", and tells him how he has come to exchange the defence of the poor and the persecuted for the defence of pimps, thieves and pederasts.

His life was originally devoted to outwardly virtuous self-interest. He would help blind men across the road, give lifts during transport strikes and readily give alms to beggars, until virtue became its own delight : he had arrived at the ". . . apex of the pyramid of ambition where virtue needs no reward other than itself". (p. 30).

He exercised his profession of advocacy partly from an instinctive dislike of judges, and partly because of the happiness it allowed him. He was assured in his judgements of human nature and felt his interest in the welfare of others to be the best means of determining his own composure.

One evening, on the Pont des Arts, after a particularly successful day (a blind man, a case won, a brilliant discourse to some friends on the hardness of heart shown by the ruling classes) he was shocked in his moment of exaltation by a laugh, the source of which he could not discern.

This first awakening led to a certain realization of his own need to dominate others : he used women for the pleasure of control and decision over their emotional destinies : "Every man needs slaves just as he must have fresh air to breathe". (p. 54); "As you must know, the truth is that every intelligent man dreams of becoming a gangster and ruling society by violence alone". (p. 66).

On another, later occasion, while crossing the Pont Royal, he passed a girl who threw herself into the Seine. He made no attempt to save her, or to call for help; he merely walked on. He was haunted by a curious guilt, and discovered himself to be the focus of human enmity—a man envied for his apparent happiness and the "mental lucidity" his friends were accustomed to praise him for. He gradually destroyed his reputation and sought for love, chastity and, finally, debauchery in the arms of women—the sole remnants of "an earthly paradise". He grew in the realization and practice of self-love; for debauchery implies a lack of obligation to others.

While on a liner with one of these women, he saw a piece of flotsam on the water and believed, for a moment, that it was the girl whom he had abandoned.

In Amsterdam, he now seeks to fix his presumed guilt on those whom he meets in his rôle of "judge-penitent" or as a bar-fly: "I am the end and the beginning: I am come to announce the law. To put it briefly, I am a judge-penitent" (p. 136).

The monological structure of the novel is a comment on language as a means of searching and analysing the conscience. Clamence is an unusually good stylist, given to the utterance of ironic aphorisms on human conduct which recall French moralists such as La Rochefoucauld. But Clamence directs the irony against himself and the entire human race. The straightness of execution in the book covers an intentional moral ambiguity: Clamence gives an assumed name; he was an amateur actor; he feels himself to be fully realized in his abandonment of conventional charity. The very purity of style is necessary to prevent the novel itself suffering from the disintegration of values that it presents: "Man is like that, my friend; he has two faces: he can't love without loving himself". (p. 41). *The Fall* is a poignant illustration of the contention that the novel is the art-form of a world "abandoned by God". The ultimate irony of the book is our inability to trust the narrator and, through his stated identification with the reader, ourselves.

But we are sure of something: that Clamence has fallen and that he is falling. He does so throughout the novel, as Milton's Satan continues to fall throughout *Paradise Lost*; in both cases the final assurance is the most disturbing: each refuses his particular paradise to become a "new pope living among the persecuted". (p. 145). We can now hear the man talking on the other side of the glass pane in the telephone booth;[2] but it is as if the booth were metamorphosed into a lift, in which we

[2] cf. *The Myth of Sisyphus*.

realize that we also are descending, having, through complicity, refused the ascent to the heights.

The central paradoxes of the novel are Clamence's adoption of the dual rôle of judge and penitent, and his acceptance of the "greatest of human torments" which is "to be judged without the law". (p. 136).

In its illustration of these paradoxes, *The Fall* uses more literary allusions than either of Camus' two previous *récits*. The bar-owner—the "gorilla"—is associated with the porter of Dante's ninth circle. Jean-Baptiste Clamence is, as his name implies, an unworthy successor to St John the Baptist: he bears witness only to darkness and moral chaos; he is also a traitor like those in the last book of the *Inferno*: "Have you noticed that the concentric canals of Amsterdam are like the circles of hell? The bourgeois hell, of course, stocked with bad dreams . . . Here, we are in the last circle." (p. 120).

Murky Amsterdam becomes a fit setting for the spiritual Limbo of the false prophet; for he is not vouchsafed the grace of Purgatory: "You will remember that Dante allows the presence of neutral angels in the quarrel between God and Satan. He puts them in Limbo, a kind of ante-room to his Hell. That's what we are, my friend." (p. 98). The Zuyder-Zee is a "Dead Sea" and the doves will never descend upon this shadowy waste.

The Christian references in *The Fall* are more explicit than those in *The Plague*. Clamence is a prophet proper to our times—those of confused moral imperatives; where the means is employed for an unknown end, and where life seems dead: "the universal effacement: nothingness visible". (p. 86).

The people of Holland are swans—illusions of an impossible and romantic paradise, forsaken by Clamence when he refused the baptismal water beneath the bridge where a girl was drowning: "Holland is a dream, a dream of gold and smoke, smokier in the daytime and more golden by night; night and day this dream is peopled with Lohengrins like these, dreamily passing by on their black bicycles with the high handlebars, funereal swans riding unceasingly through the whole country, around the waters and along the canals". (pp. 18-19). But it is the beauty

of a wasteland that attracts him in this world where the rain
falls as if to announce a second Flood: "How beautiful the
canals are this evening! I like the air wafted from stagnant
waters, the scent of the dead leaves soaking in the canal and
the funereal odour that rises from the barges filled with flowers."
(pp. 52-53).

He now preaches the baptism of guilt, which he would extend
to all men. For the laughter was heard and the death was
observed by Clamence as he stood on a symbolic bridge separat-
ing innocence from experience. He can be a prophet only now
that he has forsaken action and left the city of men.

At times, Clamence might be Camus himself commenting
upon his earlier flights of lyricism and, ironically, castigating
himself for his advocacy of sensual human pleasure. But Clamence also shows the end of a civilization: the desertion by a
man of some culture of a belief both in human simplicity and
in reason; he will have "no more books, no more vain trap-
pings". (p. 141).

The more schematic allegory of human suffering that we
find in *The Plague* has been abandoned. We have, in its place
possibilities of direct identification with what Camus saw as
major refusals of our time: political duplicity towards the persecuted, a refusal to join the resistance against evil and suffering. Whether or not he did so for personal pleasure, Clamence
did defend "noble causes"; but, like many intellectuals who had
followed the dream of romantic communism, he has abandoned
even the practice of charity. He also refused to join the Resistance in war-time France, and drank the water of a suffering
fellow prisoner in an internment camp. He has become a false
prophet who should return to the world of men; but he commits
the sin of presuming to do God's work of judgement for Him
and therefore denies himself real brotherhood with other men :
"I pity without giving absolution; I understand without for-
giving; and, above all, I feel that I am adored". (p. 165). Now
he has only the "bitter water of his baptism"; he is "without
rebellion", and denies the usefulness of the good physician.[3]

[3] Rieux, in *The Plague*.

But Clamence has sought out a fit place of guilt for his prophetic task: this Limbo is also the scene of one of the twentieth century's main crimes against humanity—the persecution of the Jews: "I live in the Jewish quarter, or so it was called until our Nazi brethren cleared it out a little. And what a clearance! Seventy-five thousand Jews deported or murdered: that is vacuum-cleaning! I admire such application and methodical patience! If you haven't any character, you really have to have a method." (p. 16).

Here, he is able to oppose cynicism to romanticism; for Camus' portrait is designed so that the reader will recognize part of himself—and all men—in Clamence. The theme is universal: the moral countenance of an immoral age. For Clamence, his paradoxically moral phrasing of an immoral mission is justified because "the order of the world is . . . ambiguous". He has no reason to be "good". Originally, he was conventionally good because of the approbation he received from others; his experience with the girl-suicide showed him that he was unable always to be good. He realized the imperfections in the practice of human charity. The paradise that he has lost, and whose attainability he suggests with his exotic images, is one where all men are naturally good—or where they have some suasion to do good deeds. But now he must have absolute justice or absolute guilt: even Christ, he says, was to a certain extent guilty in causing the deaths of the innocent babes slain by Herod. Clamence falls from grace and from the assurance of grace; his cynical acceptance of guilt for human anguish (the murder of the Jews) is accompanied by a withdrawal from the sun and from the possibility of freedom-in-innocence.

Like the renegade priest-missionary in *Exile and the Kingdom*, he accepts a new fetish: brute domination, though he must despize it. He now defends the pimps and thieves who prey upon society.

We may read *The Fall* as Camus' statement of the complex nature of human motivation; as a more ironical comment on the simply defined type of *The Plague*—the secular saint. Perhaps *The Fall* was Camus' introduction to a more complex definition of human values—the awakening of a conscience rather than the awakening of consciousness.

This voice crying in the sombre wilderness of Amsterdam calls the reader to a recognition of the bottomless heart of evil in all men; it calls him to an "unusual lucidity" : "The day I found out, I was granted lucidity; I received all the wounds at once and lost my strength at one go. The entire universe began to laugh around me then". (p. 94); it calls him also to a universal condemnation : ". . . we cannot affirm the innocence of any man, whereas we can certainly state that all men are guilty". (p. 127).

There is no moral law; yet man is collectively guilty. This judgement on the human condition prevents Clamence from making an existential choice; like all men, he is guilty of the ultimate sin, he exists; like Lear's hand, everyone "smells of mortality". It is as if the knowledge of universal evil had deprived Clamence of the *freedom* to choose virtue. He is like the philosophers and politicians whom Camus decries in *The Rebel* for their ignoring of practical moral demands in order to construct a metaphysics, or build, at the expense of humanity, an eternal city on earth. By water and at night, man has been called from his dwelling within himself to an action that would enable him effectively to live with others; and he has refused. The false prophet denies the individual freedom of all men because he would deny his own right and duty to make a moral choice. He denies what Camus believed : "that my heart can intervene and dictate my happiness up to a certain limit where the world can then bring it about or destroy it".[4]

Several extreme statements are paradoxically reconciled in *The Fall*. It is possible that Camus was writing a subtle condemnation of the Christian conception of an all-merciful God; it is equally possible that he was moving towards a more Christian position. Whatever the precise personal direction of his thought may have been, *The Fall* is a demand for the assurance of justice; it enables us to endorse Sartre's judgement of Camus : "This Descartes of the Absurd refused to leave the

[4] *Carnets*, p. 96.

safe ground of morality and venture on the uncertain paths of practicality. We sensed this and we also sensed the conflicts he kept hidden, for ethics, taken alone, both requires and condemns revolt."[5]

[5] Jean-Paul Sartre: "Tribute to Albert Camus", *The Reporter*, 4 February 1964, p. 34.

7. *Camus as a Dramatist*

THE DEVELOPMENT of Camus' plays runs parallel to that of his novels: both plays and novels have the same direction. It would not be an arbitrary judgement to make a distinction between the *absurd* and the *rebellious* plays of Camus.

I. THE THEATRE OF THE ABSURD

In June 1944, in the immediate post-Liberation period, Camus' second play *Le Malentendu (Cross Purpose)* was staged at the Théâtre des Mathurins. *Caligula* was produced at the Théâtre Hébertot in September 1945.

Cross Purpose

A mother and her daughter, Martha, run an isolated inn in the Moravian countryside. When a rich visitor arrives, they give him a sleeping-draught, rob him and then throw him in the river. One day Jan, the son who had left home twenty years before, knocks at the door. They do not recognize him (for he has concealed his identity), and he joins the others in the river.

This wasteland inhabited by criminals is our absurd universe; Jan, the stranger who knocks at the door, is the question asked; the corpse that rots as it lies pressed to the sluice-gate is the answer given.

The nature of the universe: We are no longer confronted

with the monotonous and mechanical world of *The Outsider*, but with the hideousness of anarchy and crime. The course of everyday life is peaceful, despite its monotony; the repose of the automaton is pleasurable. But here, on the stage, we see a closed universe: a world of claustrophobia with no horizon. The mud and rain of the landscape have nothing to offer those who long for another life. Martha kills in order to escape from this setting; so that she may see the ocean again and feel the sun upon her. At the same time, she adds to the horror of her environment by emphasizing one of its aspects—destruction. Martha and her mother have fed long upon the fruit of destruction:

THE MOTHER: But this world itself is meaningless and I've a right to say so if anyone has: I've tasted everything in it, from creation to slaughter.

The question asked: The son knocks at the door. He is a stranger to this world. Until now he has enjoyed happiness in a sun-lit land with the woman he loves. But his happiness was blind and now he wants an answer to his problem:

JAN *(he is talking to his wife, Maria)*: It's true that a man needs happiness, but he also has to find his true place in life.

He will seek this place by means of truths that, for him, seem to point out the way:

JAN: And I think that returning to my own country and bringing happiness to those I love, will help me to find that place.

But he suspects that there is no answer, that the door will not open and that his ideal is refused him by reality.

Alone, in the bedroom of the inn, where his wife refuses to join him, he is afraid: "It's always like this in hotel bedrooms: a lonely man always finds the evenings difficult to get through. Now I can feel my old dread again, down there, in the pit of my stomach like an open wound that each movement irritates. It's a dread I know well. It's everlasting solitude I'm afraid of—afraid there'll be no answer."

There is no answer, except murder. The request for a land

of one's own is answered with a diseased soil: violence is offered in place of peace, and solitude instead of love. This is the sum of Martha's savage address to Jan's wife:

MARTHA : The fool! He has what he wanted, now he's found the woman he was looking for [his mother]. Now we've all got what's decreed for us. So just be clear about it : there's no home-land and there's no peace—none for him, none for us, none when you're alive and none when you're dead. *(She gives a scornful laugh.)* You can't call that your homeland, can you; the dank, bleak soil where you end up, feeding blind worms . . . It's all a fraud, I tell you. What is the point of all those great human longings, those cries from the heart? Why cry out for the sea or for love? It's absolutely pointless. Your husband knows the answer now : that dreadful house in the earth where in the end we shall all be laid side by side.

In fact, this event is not a chance occurrence or an accidental misunderstanding, but the necessary image of our human condition, which is one of solitude and love abused. Martha wants to destroy Maria's last illusion and to bring her to despair in showing her that there is *no way out.*

MARTHA : Before I leave you for ever, I think I still have some-thing to do. Now I must make you despair.

MARIA *(staring at her, in horror)* : Oh, leave me alone! Get out and leave me alone!

MARTHA : I am going to leave you. It will be a relief for me, too : I can't bear you with your love and your tears. But I do not want to die leaving you under the impression that you are right, that love isn't pointless and that all this has been no more than an accident. You see, it's now that we're in the normal order of life. That's what I have to show you.

MARIA : What order of life?

MARTHA : Where no one is ever recognized.

Maria also seeks an answer; although Jan is dead, she con-tinues to search and turns to a God who is Mercy :

MARIA *(she cries out)* : Oh, Father in heaven, I cannot live in this desert . . . Have pity on me, look down on me! Lord, hear me! . . .

A character who has been silent until this point in the play now gives the answer: 'No!' The curtain drops.

The barren heart: This is the key of truth that opens the door of the world for us. Martha is an incarnation of spiritual barrenness reacting to experience. Hers is the inner dryness of the unfeeling soul that asks how one can live with the desire to love.

MARIA *(almost abstractedly)*: But why did you do it, why?
MARTHA: What right have you to ask me that?
MARIA *(screaming)*: Because I love him!
MARTHA: What does *love* mean?

Cross Purpose is more of a "demonstration" than a play. Nevertheless, the dialogue is alive and powerful. The character of the mother—the murderess weary of her crimes—retains the power to move us, despite the lack of psychological truth. Jan and Martha are more abstract; they are symbolic representations of the "question" and the "answer". The voice of Martha, with its strange precision reminiscent of *The Myth of Sisyphus*, is heard too often. But she, too, sometimes assumes a certain human reality when she declares her longing for pleasure, or when she tries to drive Maria to despair. But Camus's theatrical success is yet to come. Over a year later, the curtain rises on *Caligula*.

Caligula[1]

The style of the play is brisk: the dialogue consists of rapid series of statements and retorts. Philosophy appears to have been forgotten, yet philosophy gives the language of the play its sharp edge. *Caligula* is *The Myth of Sisyphus* in action: it shows the hero of the absurd carrying out his programme. He is the absurd man allowed an empire as his field of activity.

The discovery of the absurd: This is the starting point. Drusilla, the wife whom Caligula loved, is dead: "I know now that nothing endures! To know that!" The veil has been rent: "Men die; and they know no happiness".

[1] Written in 1938, four or five years before *Cross Purpose*.

Liberation: All values disappear. Caligula acquires complete freedom, and is determined to exercise it : "There is no limit to my freedom : today and for the rest of my life".

The exercise of liberty: The play is essentially concerned with this, the source of its lively, staccato style. *Caligula* is both a tragedy—the discovery of the absurd has a disruptive effect— and a comic attack on false gods.

The comedy: The patricians, these Roman dignitaries, have to undergo various ignominies : they must write poems, give an offering to Caligula disguised as Venus, surrender their wives to the Emperor, and so on . . . They are grotesque automatons; they show us Camus as a comic author.

The tragedy: Caligula pulls the strings of his puppets with the tragic aim of destroying the established order : not only that of his empire but the order of absolute morality and even the course of nature : Caesonia [Caligula's former mistress] implores Caligula to listen :

CAESONIA : There's good and bad, great and despicable, justice and injustice. I swear to you that none of these will ever change.

CALIGULA : What's the use of my fantastic power if I can't change the set order of things, if I can't make the sun set in the east . . .

CAESONIA : You can't make the sky anything other than the sky; you can't stop a handsome face becoming ugly or a man's heart unfeeling.

CALIGULA *(with increasing excitement)* : I want to bring the sky down into the sea, to mix ugliness and beauty, to bring laughter forth from anguish.

For Caligula, the exercise of liberty means that he must *destroy* the world himself. His power does not extend that far, but he has almost complete control over men. Caligula even goes so far as to kill the woman he loves :

CAESONIA *(screaming)* : You cannot deny love !

CALIGULA *(in a fierce rage)* : Love, Caesonia ! *(He takes her by the shoulders and presses her against him.)* I have discovered that it means nothing. *(He strangles her, saying)* No, no tenderness. We must put an end to it, dear Caesonia !

Understanding Caligula: He kills because he longs for a *meaningful* life. The human condition is absurd, since Drusilla is dead; therefore some other means must be found of quenching our thirst for truth; the *impossible* must be conquered amidst the ruins of our world. Murder is the "deviation of an impulse"[2] towards unity and eternity.

Caligula must not be judged as the frightened patricians, jealous of their privileges, judge him; Scipio views him correctly, for he sees that a high ideal has been distorted.

The theatre of the absurd is more audacious than *The Myth of Sisyphus*: it describes the ruinous consequences of the discovery made one day "at the corner of a street", for it is a theatre of violence and of murder. Nevertheless, even in *Cross Purpose* and *Caligula*, the presence of some characters shows that this is not merely a depiction of extremely painful mistakes.[3] In other words, just as Caligula is given an empire, Camus is given the theatre to carry out his experiments; but that does not mean that he approves of the results. He allows the absurd logic to take its way, observes the results—which are crime or madness—and then looks for the fault : the tragic flaw. *Caligula* is a research laboratory for the theoretician of *The Rebel*.

II. THE THEATRE OF REBELLION

L'État de Siège (State of Siege) was produced for the first time in October 1948 by the Compagnie Madeleine Renaud—Jean-Louis Barrault. A year later *The Just* was staged at the Théâtre Hébertot (December 1949).

State of Siege

Now the setting is the city of Cadiz and all its inhabitants : fishermen, merchants and dignitaries. Preceded by the sinister

[2] cf. *The Rebel*.

[3] The mother, in *Cross Purpose*, discovers the value of love, through suffering: "I now have one certainty—a mother's love for her son".

Caligula himself realizes that he has taken the wrong path : "I have not followed the proper road and I have come to nothing. My freedom is not true liberty." He recognizes that his friend Scipio is right.

forewarning of a comet, the Plague appears—in the guise of the actor Pierre Bertin. The struggle begins between orderly, *mechanical* death and rebellion inspired by love and freedom. The philosophical interest of the play must be distinguished from the dramatic interest.

The play has considerable philosophical interest; the reasons are as follows:

—all the themes of Camus' philosophy of rebellion are present;

—they are connected, contrasted and carefully fused with one another.

State of Siege has both the unity proper to a philosophical system and that proper to a concrete representation of such a system.

The main characters: The insane Nada is the incarnation of complete negation; Victoria represents individual happiness, the Plague stands for murder and Diego for rebellion in the service of men . . .

The dramatic interest is weak, since the characters never really come alive.

The city of Cadiz is symbolic: it is not a real city for its inhabitants are ideas personified rather than living human beings. The play does not take place in Spain but in any country in the world.

The argument touched off by an article of Gabriel Marcel[4] is pointless. "Why Spain?" But the setting of the play is not really Spain, but an imaginary country; this is a *myth* and not a piece of contemporary reportage: "In short it was a question of creating a myth which would be intelligible to every spectator" (Camus' Preface to *State of Siege*). Spain is of little importance; it is not the target of the play's attack, but merely a convenient means for the author to present certain ideas to the audience.

[4] Camus' reply to the notice of the dramatic critic of *Les Nouvelles Littéraires* is the essay "Pourquoi l'Espagne?" *(Why Spain?)*. He has chosen to refer more directly to Spain and the dictatorship of Franco than to Russia and communist oppression, but the play is an attack on totalitarianism in general.

But Camus, in *State of Siege*, is unfaithful to his art and his aesthetic ideas and therefore cannot move us. The essential element of reality is missing. The spectator is presented with a certain pattern of beauty; but it is the beauty of a myth, not that of the street he has just left for the theatre and which he will see again in a short time.

Camus has not made use of the *historical* Spain; the hope he allows the inhabitants of the city is not the living hope of the men who fought for *rebellion* in real life; the Spain of André Malraux's *L'Espoir*[5] *(Hope)* must be preferred to the myth of *State of Siege*, which is outside time and space.

The style—except for some of the lines spoken by Victoria— is artificial, for the first time in Camus' works :

The *irony* is too obviously laid on and does not arise directly from the situations.

The *dialogue* is a series of exchanges of ideas, and not a series of contacts between living characters.

The *poetry* is obviously manufactured—an unusual phe- nomenon for the prose poet of *Les Noces (Nuptials)*. The lyrical element is forced and description becomes mere enumeration; Camus succumbs to the temptation of local colour.

In short, *State of Siege* is an interesting experiment,[6] but it appears to lack the essential elements of a dramatic success— as its stage history proves.

Les Justes (The Just)

Camus takes his subject from history, as he indicates in the programme sold at the doors of the Théâtre Hébertot before the performance : "In February 1905, in Moscow, a group of terrorists—all members of the Socialist Revolutionary Party—

[5] It is possible to see in "Pourquoi l'Espagne" a kind of atonement for *State of Siege* on Camus' part, for in this essay he has, in fact, joined Andreé Malraux in making direct reference to the *historical* Spain.

[6] "This is not a play with a conventional structure, but a 'spectacle', the declared intention of which is to combine all forms of dramatic expression from the lyrical monologue to the collective theatre, together with the incidental use of mime, simple dialogue, farce and a musical score." *Foreword.*

plan to assassinate the Czar's uncle, the Grand Duke Sergei, by throwing a bomb into his carriage. This attempt and the particular circumstances that preceded and followed it are the subject of *The Just*. Although some of the situations in the play may seem very extraordinary, they are based on historical fact. This does not mean, as you will see, that *The Just* is an historical play. But all my characters existed in real life and behaved as I portray them . . . I have even given Kaliayev, the hero, the name he actually bore."[7]

The conflict between the demands of the revolution and those of the heart is the basis of the play. Stepan is opposed to Kaliayev.

Stepan

Any means is good if it allows the revolution to triumph : lies, deception or assassination. Above all assassination and the throwing of a bomb . . . Ultimately, Stepan, bearing the marks of gaol and the knout, and filled with hatred, succumbs to nihilism : "This world must be completely devastated". The love for which he is prepared to fight will come *later*; but Stepan does not go beyond hatred—that is his reality.

Kaliayev

He is fighting for the sake of life and not for death; for the emancipation of slaves and not for an inhuman form of justice; for the present and not for the future; for his human brothers and not for a paradise in the far-distant future. For these reasons he refuses to base the revolution on dishonour, injustice and murder : "But my love is extended to those who are living at the present moment on the same earth that I inhabit : those are the men I respect. I am fighting for them, and for them I am willing to die. I shall not strike my brothers in the face for the sake of a city of happiness set in the far-distant future and of whose building I cannot be certain. I shall not add to living injustice for the sake of a dead justice. (In a lower voice, but

---

[7] *The Just* is paralleled in *The Rebel* by the historical study of the "sensitive murderers".

firmly). Brothers, I want to speak to you frankly and to tell you something at least that the most simple of our peasants could tell you : to kill children is contrary to honour. And if, one day, when I am still alive, the revolution should leave the path of honour, I shall abandon the revolution."

He refuses to kill children and so he refuses to throw his bomb into the carriage of the Grand Duke, because on the day set for the assassination he is accompanied by his nephews :

KALIAYEV : Look at me, brothers; look at me, Boria. I am not a coward—I didn't flinch from my task. I didn't expect them to be there. Everything happened too quickly. These two serious little faces, and this awful weight in my hand. And I had to throw it at them. Just like that. Straight at them. No, I couldn't do it !

In the name of efficacious action, Stepan condemns Kaliayev's withdrawal from action. What is the life of a child when set against the triumph of the revolution !

STEPAN : I have too little sentiment to bother with this foolishness. When we resolve to forget about children, then we shall be masters of the world and the revolution will triumph.

Later he again says that there are no limits. But Dora, who prepares the bombs, affirms in the name of love : "Even in the midst of destruction, there is an order, there are limits."[8]

Dora and Kaliayev

They are in love; at the same time they are both rent by an inner conflict. The demands of happiness are in conflict with the demands of justice. The service of others is opposed to a love that sets two human being apart from others. The service of others is austere indeed and dries up the springs of the heart, for it demands assassination and leads to the scaffold. In the middle of the process, Dora asks for a halt to be called, for a

---

[8] The same Dora will be severely affected by the death of the Grand Duke. *No* destruction should be tolerated by a soul that knows the truth—this is the deep truth she represents. Kaliayev himself feels that he can atone only through his own death.

few moments given up to sentiment: "My mind dwells on it, do you see: the sun shines, heads are softly bent, the heart is rid of pride and our arms are open. Oh, Janek, if only one could forget, even for an hour, the shameful anguish of this world and finally let oneself go. Only one little egotistical hour—can you imagine it?"

We call to mind the conflict that affects the characters of *The Plague*—a conflict that they are unable to resolve. Here, where service to others involves violence; where happiness is set not against *sympathy* but an inhuman form of justice, a solution is made clear: human love through suffering and condemnation to death: "It's easy, it's much, much easier to die for one's contradictions than to live them," cries Dora. And Kaliayev, from his prison-cell, asks: "But isn't it already possible to imagine two human beings renouncing all happiness and loving one another in the midst of pain without allowing themselves any other union than that of pain?" Dora follows Kaliayev in his fate: in this way the two aspects of truth that divide his heart will be united.

Camus' plays vary in style, from the dryness of *Cross Purpose* to the painful complexity of *The Just*; but they offer us the same movement as the theoretical or fictional works. The same point is reached: the defence of truly human values. Camus' plays use the means proper to the theatre—the *peripeteia* of plot and conflicting characterization—to demonstrate that truth is to be sought not in tranquillity and peace, but in contradiction.

8. Lyricism in Camus' Works

POETRY IS to be found throughout Camus' works. His early essays (*L'Envers et l'endroit*—*Betwixt and Between*—in 1937 and *Noces*—*Nuptials*—published in 1938 but written in its first form in 1936) are lyrical works, and the poetical tone is to be found in his plays and novels and sometimes even in his theoretical writings. Poetry is the unchangeable and living texture of Camus' inspiration. It precedes the experience of the absurd,[1] and is also used to celebrate its discovery. It is the "irremovable road home" in Camus' life.[2]

I. ALIENATION

Travelling lays the soul bare: "The price of the journey is exacted by fear. It shatters a kind of ornamental framework within us. You can't cheat any longer, or hide behind office or workshop hours (hours against which we protest so strongly and which give us so sure a protection against the pain of solitude). Therefore I have always wanted to write novels in which my heroes would say: 'What should I be without my office

---

[1] "Though I was born poor, I was born under a happy sky in a natural setting with which one feels in union, unalienated. So I did not begin in redundancy but in fullness." "Three Interviews" in *Actuelles*, p. 225.

[2] See "Return to Tipasa", written in 1953 (in *l'Été (Summer)*, Gallimard, 1954). See also the Preface to the new edition of *Betwixt and Between* (Gallimard, 1958), where Camus states that this first essay remains central to his work. ("I know that the source of my inspiration is to be found in *Betwixt and Between*.")

hours?' or : 'My wife is dead, but luckily I have all that cor-
respondence to see to for tomorrow.' Travelling deprives us of
this refuge : far from our family and friends, our own language
and our supports and deprived of our masks (you don't know
how much the tram ticket costs—everything's like that), we live
an entirely external existence."[3]

Simultaneously, the world is revealed to us; no longer is it
hidden from us by the screen of habit : ". . . we allow every
creature and every object its miraculous, individual value. A
woman dancing for the sheer fun of it, a bottle on the table,
seen behind a curtain . . ."

The voyage within therefore corresponds to a journey through
space : it takes the soul out of its *internal setting* and transfers it
to the external world; it is a movement from the bleakness of
everyday life to the rich life of sensation.

The shock of awareness, one day at a street-corner, provides
the necessary impulsion to make the same journey. Like the
traveller on the roadway, consciousness abandons its mechanical
aids and faces the world. It requires no journey in space; it is
the appearance of its own town that changes, for the sake of
consciousness : Camus celebrates Palma and Prague, but he is
able to do the same for Oran or Algiers.

II. POETRY IN THE WORLD

The song inspired by the experience of the absurd is some-
what harsh; it does not come from the heart, but from the world
itself; the poet has cast his individuality aside to confront the
world of phenomena; he identifies himself with the world
—he becomes a tree, a stone or the sky. The lyrical prose
of Camus is largely an attempt to express this identification; it
is *sensory*, since through it the poet seeks to depict the union of
the human body with the whole body of the universe : it celebrates its "marriage with the world". Thus Camus describes
the ruins of Tipasa, in Africa, which overlook the sea :[4] "In

---

[3] "Amour de vivre" in *L'Envers et l'Endroit*.
[4] "Noces à Tipasa" *(The Wedding at Tipasa)* in *Noces (Nuptials)*.

springtime, Tipasa is inhabited by the gods and the gods speak in the sun and the scent of wormwood, the silver-plated sea, the natural blue of the sky, the flower-covered ruins and the light poured out on the heaps of stones. Sometimes, the country-side seems black with sunlight. One's eyes try in vain to grasp anything else besides the drops of light and the colours that tremble on the edges of one's eyelashes. The thick perfume of aromatic plants rasps the throat and seems suffocating in the great heat. Far off in the countryside, the black mass of the Chenoua is hardly visible where it rises in the hills around the village and moves forward with a sure and powerful motion to cast itself into the sea." Camus' lyricism is not that of a spectator but of an actor sharing in the variegated rhythms of nature; this gives the few pages of *Nuptials* and *Betwixt and Between* their diverse range, whether Camus is describing the sea or the sky, the wildness of the African hills or the hills about Florence . . .

The colours are unmixed, applied in thick washes, and con-trasted : there are no subtle effects. Camus' verbal palette is reminiscent of some fauvist paintings. He is not afraid to write : "We enter a world of yellow and blue . . ." A few pages later, he says : "I would describe it thus : "This is red, this is blue and this is green; this is the sea, this is the mountain, and these are the flowers'."[5]

Camus is an actor, sensitive to the "tumultuous sighs of the world"; but he is also a spectator when necessary, in order to enjoy a landscape or the evening adequately : Camus at Florence is the poet of silence and delicate colours. Emotion takes the place of sensation and exhilaration is tempered with melancholy : "In Florence, I climbed up above the Boboli gardens . . ."[6] he also visits Palma and its monastery : "By the little well of the monastery of San Francisco, I watched the flights of pigeons wheeling by . . ."[7]

The tenderness that Dora called for in the midst of murder,

[5] "The Wedding at Tipasa".
[6] "The Desert", in *Nuptials*.
[7] "Amour de vivre".

and which is so seldom met with in the pages of Camus the writer on the absurd, is encountered in some pages, here and there. These pages are few, but some of them are to be found even in *The Outsider* and its world of monotony, and in *The Plague*, where the world has become tragic.

III.   LIFE AND DEATH

Nevertheless, the poet does not lose his lucidity: he never forgets the inescapable reality in the world—which is death. A third dimension is added to tenderness and sensation. Perceptive despair is joined with exhilaration and love. The rising of consciousness to the surface of things is not an escape from time and an encounter with an eternal present. Camus never speaks of "extra-temporal essences", for the experience of Proust has always been denied him. Nature does not satisfy the longing for unity that fills the human consciousness; on the contrary, nature scorns this longing and rejects consciousness. Nature has nothing to offer us, since it is completely foreign to us. The traveller escapes from his particular stage-set and discovers the world and its alien nature: "This world escapes us, as it becomes itself again".[8] The poet tastes the beauty of things, but it is an *inhuman* beauty: in the very moment of his discovery of the world, the poet encounters death.

All real experience brings one face to face with death: this is the basic consideration in Camus' work. Learn to know life as it really is; lead a full life—of sensation or of emotion, as the case may be—but remember that a bitter penalty is exacted as you live; you will know your inescapable fate, which is death: "You cannot rejoice in life, without despairing of life".[9]

Camus' lyrical prose therefore has its due place in his works. It is structurally necessary, because it is one of the fruits of the experience of the absurd.

Camus' "poetry" is a particular and beautiful testimony to the unique quality of his thought.

[8] *The Myth of Sisyphus*, p. 29.
[9] "Amour de vivre".

Conclusion

THE MAIN quality of Camus' thought is therefore its concern with a *dualism* : the dualism of life and death, of "tenderness" and "justice", and of love and hatred. Camus simultaneously denies and affirms : his thought is an unceasing attempt to secure moderation; to maintain equilibrium between contrary and exclusive terms.

But, more important still, and in a less abstract manner, it represents a continual transition from the one to the other.

"Retour à Tipasa" *(Return to Tipasa)*, in the collection *L'Été*, published in 1952, demonstrates this; Camus returns to the African hillside he had once celebrated in *Nuptials* and, in this description of "time regained", looks back on the course of his own life, which is in itself a history of equilibrium between acceptance and rejection.

First of all there is the acceptance of adolescence in contact with the sensual beauty of the world : "I had begun with fullness". Afterwards comes the rejection of a man thrown into the conflicts of his own time : "Then came the barbed wire; and by that I mean tyrannies, war, police forces and the time of revolt".

But the time of acceptance has come again. Here is Tipasa in all its former purity—even more pure still, like the first breaking of the day : "And in the glorious December light, as happens only once or twice in lives which, afterwards, can consider themselves filled to overflowing, I found exactly what I had come to look for . . ." : the silence and the light.

Camus returns to the world of men and its conflicts. But the acceptance experienced at Tipasa will be enclosed within rejection; it is necessary to remember the wearisome truth that neither of the two terms can be excluded.

We should nevertheless note the extreme movements that unceasingly threaten to disturb the balance of Camus' desires. "Return to Tipasa" is a basic statement of acceptance; it is a moment of profound understanding that appears finally to escape the dualism of acceptance and rejection. On the other hand, *La Chute (The Fall)*, published in 1956, is the "No!" of Clamence, the "judge-penitent" who is engaged in a pitiless self-examination of his own moments of acceptance. The light of Tipasa gives way to the misty lights of Amsterdam.

The character of Clamence brings us the same doubt we encountered in *The Myth of Sisyphus*. But it is not related to the ideals of the man caught in the slumber of everyday existence; there is an implied reference to the ideals experienced in *The Plague*. The morality of rebellion has produced its own particular pharisee; a new purification, that of the intellect, is needed. Simultaneously, excessive doubt overwhelms all else and gives Clamence a sardonic twist, and the entire narrative its peculiarly sarcastic tone.

Camus' works define this state of equilibrium between acceptance and rejection; they are an unflagging statement of these two irreconcilable attitudes: paradoxically, they also persuade us that we must try to unite them.

I. WORKS BY CAMUS

A. FICTION

L'Étranger. (Récit), Gallimard, 1942. (*The Outsider*, trans. into English by Stuart Gilbert, with a Preface by Cyril Connolly, Hamish Hamilton, 1946.)

La Peste. (Chronique), Gallimard, 1947. (*The Plague*, trans. by Stuart Gilbert, Hamish Hamilton, 1948.)

La Chute. (Récit), Gallimard, 1956. (*The Fall*, trans. by Justin O'Brien, Hamish Hamilton, 1957.)

L'Exil et le Royaume. (Nouvelles), Gallimard, 1957. (*Exile and the Kingdom*, trans. by Justin O'Brien, Hamish Hamilton, 1958.) A collection of six powerful short stories by Camus.

The English translations listed above are also to be found in:
The Collected Fiction of Albert Camus, Hamish Hamilton, 1960.

Volume I of a collection of Camus' works in French is:
Albert Camus: Théatre, récits, nouvelles, ed. R. Quilliot, Gallimard, 1962.

B. ESSAYS ETC.

L'Envers et l'endroit (Betwixt and Between), Charlot, 1937. Five essays by Camus. Re-published, with an important preface, Gallimard, 1958.

Noces (Nuptials), Charlot, 1938. Essays. New edition, Gallimard, 1947.

Le Mythe de Sisyphe, Gallimard, 1942. (*The Myth of Sisyphus*, trans. by Justin O'Brien, Hamish Hamilton, 1955.) This translation is accompanied by some of Camus' essays: *Summer in*

Algiers, from *Nuptials; Helen's Exile*, from *Summer; The Mino-taur*, or *The Stop at Oran*; and *Return to Tipasa*.

Lettres à un ami allemand, Gallimard, 1945. Essays. (*Letters to a German Friend*, trans. by Justin O'Brien in *Resistance, Rebellion and Death*, Hamish Hamilton, London, 1961.) This essay consists of four letters written to a German during the Occupation. The first of them appeared in the second number of *La Revue Libre*, in 1943; the second in the third number of *Cahiers de la Libération* at the beginning of 1944. The other two were written for *La Revue Libre*, but remained unpublished. They defend man's "senses" and his happiness.

Remarque sur la révolte, in the collection *L'Existence*, Gallimard, 1945. In some senses a first draft for *The Rebel*, in which some passages appear unchanged.

Actuelles: *Chroniques*, 1944-1948, Paris, Gallimard, 1950. Articles.

L'Homme Révolté, Gallimard, 1951. Essay. (*The Rebel*, trans. by Anthony Bower; preface by Sir Herbert Read, London, Hamish Hamilton, 1953. Some passages from the original work were not included in this translation.)

Actuelles: Chroniques, 1948-1953. Gallimard, 1953. Of especial interest among these articles:
A reply to André Breton, about *The Rebel*.
The letters exchanged between Camus, Sartre and F. Jeanson, are extremely violent in their tone, and throw light on the break between the two great French writers (the three letters are to be found in the number of *Les Temps Modernes* for August 1952).

L'Été, Gallimard, 1954. This collection contains essays written over a period of fifteen years (*The Minotaur, Helen's Exile*, etc. Of greatest interest: *Return to Tipasa*, in which Camus looks back on himself as he was twenty years before. These particular essays appear in *The Myth of Sisyphus*, trans. by Justin O'Brien.)

Actuelles: *Chronique algérienne, 1939-1958*, Gallimard, 1958. Articles.

Réflexions sur la peine de mort (in collaboration with Arthur Koestler and Jean Bloch-Michel) Calmann-Lévy, 1957. (Camus' contribution appears in the collection *Resistance, Rebellion and Death*, trans. by Justin O'Brien.)

Discours de Suède, Gallimard, 1958. (*Speech of Acceptance upon the Award of the Nobel Prize for Literature*, trans. by Justin O'Brien, in *Resistance, Rebellion and Death*, Hamish Hamilton, 1961.)

C. PLAYS

La Révolte des Asturies, a collective effort "Pour les amis du théâtre et du travail", Charlot, 1936.

Le Malentendu, suivi de Caligula, Gallimard, 1944. (*Caligula and Cross Purpose*, trans. by Stuart Gilbert. Preface by Camus, trans. by Justin O'Brien, Hamish Hamilton, 1948.) Revised edition; Gallimard, 1958.

L'État de Siège, Gallimard, 1948. (*Caligula and Three other Plays*, trans. by Stuart Gilbert, Hamish Hamilton, 1958, contains *State of Siege*.)

Les Justes, Gallimard, 1950. (*The Just* in *Caligula and Three other Plays*.)

D. TRANSLATIONS AND ADAPTATIONS FOR THE THEATRE

Les Esprits, by Pierre de Larivey, Gallimard, 1953.

Le Dévotion à la Croix, by Caldéron (*La devoción de la Cruz*), Gallimard, 1953.

Un Cas Intéressant, by Dino Buzatti (*Un caso clinico*), L'Avant-scène No. 4, 1955.

Requiem pour une nonne, by Faulkner (*Requiem for a Nun*), Gallimard, 1956.

Le Chevalier d'Olmédo, by Lope de Vega (*El caballero de Olmedo*), Gallimard, 1957.

Les Possédés, by Fyodor Dostoevsky, Gallimard, 1959. (*The Possessed*, trans. by Justin O'Brien, Hamish Hamilton, 1960.)

E. PREFACES TO VARIOUS WORKS

CHAMFORT, *Maximes et anecdotes*, Introduction by Albert Camus, Incidences, Monaco, 1944. The description of an absurd hero in real life.

André SALVET, *Le Combat silencieux*, prefaced by a letter from Albert Camus, le Portulan, 1945.

Pierre-Eugène CLAIRIN, *Dix estampes originales*, Prefaced by Albert Camus, Rombaldi, 1946.

René LAYNAUD, *Poésies posthumes*, Preface by Albert Camus, Gallimard, 1947. Laynaud, shot by the Germans, was a friend of Camus.

Jacques MERY, *Laissez passer mon peuple*, Preface by Albert Camus, Éditions du Seuil, 1947 (cf. also *Actuelles I*).

J. HÉON-CANONNE, *Devant la mort*, Preface by Albert Camus, Angers, Siraudeau, 1951.

Daniel MAUROT, *Contre-Amour*; Preface by Albert Camus, Editions de Minuit, 1952.

Henri GUILLOUX, *La Maison du peuple*, Grasset, 1953; an excellent preface by Camus.

Oscar WILDE, *La Ballade de la Geôle de Reading*; Introduction by Camus, 'l'artiste en prison', Falaize, 1952.

A. ROSMER, *Moscou sous Lénine; les origines du communisme*, Horay, 1953.

K. F. BIEBER, *L'Allemagne vue par les écrivains de la Résistance française*, Geneva, 1954.

Roger MARTIN DU GARD, *Oeuvres*, Gallimard, 1955 (collection de la Pléiade), Preface by Albert Camus.

Henry FAULKNER, *Requiem pour une nonne*, trans. by M. E. Coindreau, with a Preface by Albert Camus, Gallimard, 1957.

Jean GRENIER, *Les Iles*, with a Preface by Albert Camus (new edition, 1959).

F.   VARIOUS LECTURES AND ARTICLES

   (i) *Actuelles I* (listed above under B.) contains reprints of the following; The editorials in *Combat*, 1944-45.
   Le Témoin de la Liberté, address at the Salle Pleyel to an international gathering of writers.
   L'Incroyant et les Chrétiens, address to the Dominicans of the avenue de Latour-Maubourg, in Paris.

Pourquoi l'Espagne? from *Combat*, 1948; reply to an article by Gabriel Marcel.

(ii) Various uncollected articles :

L'Intelligence et l'Echafaud, special number of *Confluences,* 1943.

Remarque sur la révolte, in *Existence,* Gallimard, 1945.

Réflexions sur le christianisme, in *La vie intellectuelle,* December 1946.

Archives de la Peste, in *Cahiers de la Pléiade,* Gallimard, 1947.

Les Meurtriers délicats, in *La Table Ronde,* January 1948.

Le Meurtre et l'Absurde, in *Empédocle,* No. 1, April 1949.

Nietzsche et le Nihilisme, in *Les Temps Modernes,* August 1951.

L'Artiste et son Temps, in *Quaderni Aci,* Turin, 1955.

Lettre à Roland Barthes (regarding *La Peste*), in *Club,* February 1955.

G. OTHER BOOKS

L'Art, Dutilleul (Collection Métamorphose), 1955.

Carnets, Gallimard, 1962. (Camus' literary diary) *(Carnets: 1935-1942),* Translated by Philip Thody with an Introduction and Notes, Hamish Hamilton, 1963.

James THURBER, *La dernière fleur,* Paris, Gallimard 1952. Camus' translation of Thurber's *The Lost Flower.*

II. CRITICAL ASSESSMENTS OF CAMUS' WORKS

H. FULL-LENGTH STUDIES

Henry BONNIER, *Albert Camus ou la force d'être,* Vitté éd., 1959.

Germaine BRÉE, *Camus,* New Brunswick : Rutgers University Press, 1961.

Germaine BRÉE, *Albert Camus,* Columbia University Press, N.Y., 1964.

Jean-Claude BRISVILLE, *Camus,* "La bibliothèque idéale", Gallimard, 1959.

Robert CHAMPIGNY, *Sur un héros païen,* Gallimard, 1959.

John CRUICKSHANK, *Albert Camus and the Literature of Revolt*, London, Oxford University Press, 1959.

Anne DURAND, *Les Cas Albert Camus*, Paris, 1961.

G.-P. GÉLINAS, F.S.C., *La Liberté dans la pensée d'Albert Camus*, Fribourg, Éditions universitaires, 1965.

Thomas HANNA, *The Thought and Art of Albert Camus*, Chicago, Henry Regnery Co., 1958.

Georges HOUDIN, *Camus le juste*, Paris, 1960.

Adèle KING, *Camus*, London, Oliver and Boyd, 1964.

Robert DE LUPPÉ, *Albert Camus*, Éd. du Temps Présent, 1951.

Albert MAQUET, *Albert Camus on l'invincible Été*, Carrefour des Lettres, Éditions Debresse, 1955.

André NICOLAS, *Albert Camus, Une Philosophie de l'existence:* Presses Univ. de France, 1964.

P. NGUYEN-VAN-HUY, *La metaphysique du bonheur chez Albert Camus*, Neuchâtel, Editions de la Baconnière, 1962.

Roger QUILLIOT, *Albert Camus; La Mer et les Prisons*, Gallimard, 1956.

Nathan H. SCOTT, *Albert Camus*, London, Bowes and Bowes, 1962.

M. P.-H. SIMON, *Présence de Camus*, Brussels, La Renaissance du Livre, 1961.

Philip THODY, *Albert Camus: A Study of his Works*, London, Hamish Hamilton. 1957.

Philip THODY, *Albert Camus 1913-1960*, London, Hamish Hamilton, 1961. (The above study rewritten after Camus' death.)

Léon THOORENS, *À la rencontre d'Albert Camus*, Brussels/Paris, La Sixaine, 1946.

I. BIBLIOGRAPHY

Renate BOLLINGER, *Albert Camus: Eine Bibliographie der Literatur über ihn und sein Werk*, Cologne, 1957 (Greven Verlag).

Simone Crépin, *Albert Camus: Essai de bibliographie*, Brussels, 1960.

See also:

D. W. Alden (ed.), *Bibliography of critical and biographical references for the study of contemporary French literature, New York* (annually).

C.A.V. "Camus and *Alger Republicain* : 1938-1939", in *Yale French Studies* XXV, (Spring 1960) (a list of Camus' signed and some of his unsigned articles for the Algiers Left-wing daily).

J. ARTICLES ETC.

R. M. Albérès, *"La révolte des écrivains d'aujourd'hui"* (a chapter on Camus) Corréa, 1949.

D. Aury, "Talk with Albert Camus", in : *New York Times Book Review* for 17th February 1957.

A. J. Ayer, "Albert Camus", *Horizon*, Vol. XIII, March 1946.

G. Bataille, "Le Bonheur, le malheur et la morale d'Albert Camus", *Critique*, Vol. V, No. 33, 1949.

G. Bataille, "La Temps de la révolte", *Critique*, No. 55 and No. 56 (December, 1951 and January 1952).

Beigbeder, "Les Justes", *Esprit*, No. 164, 1950.

A. P. Bertocci, "Camus' *La Peste* and the Absurd", in *Romanic Review*, Vol. XLIX, 1958.

R. Bespaloff, "Le monde du condamné à mort", *Esprit*, Vol. XVIII No. 164, 1950.

M. Blanchot, "Le mythe de Sisyphe" and "Le Roman de l'étranger" in *Faux Pas*, Gallimard, 1943.

J. Bloch-Michel, "Albert Camus et la nostalgie de l'innocence", *Preuves*, No. 110, 1960.

P. de Boisdeffre, "Albert Camus", *Etudes*, December, 1950.

P. de Boisdeffre, "Albert Camus ou l'experience tragique", *Métamorphose de la littérature*, Vol. II (new ed. 1952).

P. de Boisdeffre, "Apparition de Camus" and "L'expérience théâtrale d'Albert Camus", *Une Histoire Vivante de la Littérature d'Aujourd'hui, 1938-1958*, Le Livre Contemporain, 1958.

Germaine Brée, "Introduction to Albert Camus," *French Studies,* Vol. IV, No. 1, 1950.

Germaine Brée, and M. Guiton, *An Age of Fiction: The French Novel from Gide to Camus,* London, 1958.

Germaine Brée (ed.), *Camus: A Collection of Critical Essays,* Englewood Cliffs (U.S.A.), 1962.

E. L. Burke, "Camus and the Pursuit of Happiness", *Thought,* Vol. XXXVII, No. 146, 1962.

Nicola Chiaromonte, "Sartre versus Camus: A Political Quarrel", *Partisan Review,* Vol. XIX, No. 6, November-December, 1952.

A. Comfort, "Albert Camus", *World Review,* November, 1949.

J. Cruickshank, "Camus' Technique in *L'Étranger*", *French Studies,* Vol. X, 1956.

J. Cruickshank, "The Art of Allegory in *La Peste*", *Symposium,* Vol. XI, 1957.

K. Douglas (ed.), *Albert Camus, Yale French Studies,* Vol. XXV, 1960.

J. Duché, "Du rocher de Sisyphe au Rocher de Brighton", *La Table Ronde,* February 1948.

G. Dumur, "Portrait d'Albert Camus", *Confluences,* No. 33, 1944.

A. Etiemble, "Peste ou péché", Les Temps modernes, Vol. III, 1947.

W. M. Frohock, "Camus: Image, Influences and Sensibility", *Yale French Studies,* Vol. II, No. 2, 1949.

A. Galpin, "Dante in Amsterdam", *Symposium,* Vol. XII, 1958.

J. Guiget, "Deux romans existentialistes: La Nausée et L'Étranger" *French Review,* Vol. XXIII, December, 1949.

D. R. Haggis, *Camus: La Peste,* Studies in French Literature, No. 9, Arnold, London, 1962.

F. Jeanson, "Albert Camus ou l'âme révoltée", *Les Temps Modernes,* Vol. VII, 1952.

F. Jeanson, "Pour tout vous dire . . .", *Les Temps Modernes,* Vol. VIII, 1952.

S. John, "Image and Symbol in the Work of Albert Camus", *French Studies*, Vol. IX, 1955.

Adèle King, "Structure and Meaning in *La Chute*" P.M.L.A., Vol. LXXVII, 1962.

R. Lâlou, "Albert Camus et la fidelité", *L'Age Nouveau*, May 1954.

K. Lansner, "Albert Camus", *Kenyon Review*, Vol. XIV, No. 4, Autumn 1952.

Q. Lauer, "Albert Camus: The Revolt against Absurdity", *Thought*, Vol. XXXV, No. 136, 1960.

E. O. Marsh (ed.), "*Les Justes* by Albert Camus", London, 1960, Introduction pp. 7-32.

G. Marcel, *L'heure théâtrale*, Plon, 1959.

H. Mason, "M. Camus and the Tragic Hero", *Scrutiny*, Vol. XIV, 1946.

H. Mason, "Albert Camus: Difficult Hope", *Scrutiny*, Vol. XIV, 1947.

C. Mauriac, "*L'Homme révolté* d'Albert Camus", *La Table ronde*, No. 48, 1951.

C. Moeller, *Littérature du XXe siècle et christianisme*, I: "Silence de Dieu" (a chapter on Camus), Casterman, 1956.

M. Mohrt, "Ethic and Poetry in the Work of Camus", *Yale French Studies*, Vol. I, 1948.

E. Mounier, "Camus Parle", *Esprit*, No. 15, 1947.

E. Mounier, "Albert Camus ou l'appel des humiliés", *L'Esprit* (Special Camus no.) January 1950.

A. Ollivier, "Albert Camus et le refus de l'Eternel", *Arche 1*, No. 6, 1944.

H. Perruchot, "Albert Camus", *Réalités*, July, 1949.

G. Picon, "Remarques sur *La Peste* d'Albert Camus", *Fontaine*, No. 61, September 1947.

R. Quilliot, "Autour d'Albert Camus et du problème socialiste", *La Revue socialiste*, April, 1948.

A. Renaud, "Quelques remarques sur le style de *l'Étranger*", *French Review*, Vol. XXX, 1957.

C. Rolo, "Albert Camus: A Good Man", *The Atlantic Monthly*, Vol. CI, No. 5, May 1958.

L. R. Rossi, "Albert Camus : The Plague of Absurdity", *Kenyon Review*, Vol. XX, 1958.

J. du Rostu, "Un Pascal sans Christ : Albert Camus", *Etudes*, Vol. CCX/VII (October 1945 and November 1945).

A. Rousseaux, "Albert Camus et la philosophie du bonheur" in : *Littérature du XXe siècle*, Albin Michel, 1949.

A. Robbe-Grillet, "Nature, humanisme, tragédie" *La Nouvelle Revue Française*, Vol. XII, 1958.

J. du Rostu, "Un Pascal sans Christ", *Etudes*, October and November 1945.

L. Roth, "Albert Camus", *Philosophy*, October 1955.

J.-P. Sartre, "Explication de *L'Étranger*" in *Situations I*, 4th ed. Paris, 1947.

J.-P. Sartre, "Réponse à Albert Camus", *Les Temps Modernes*, No. 82, 1952.

J.-P. Sartre, "Tribute to Albert Camus", *The Reporter*, 4th February 1960.

N. A. Scott, "The Modest Optimism of Albert Camus", *The Christian Scholar*, Vol. XLII, No. 4, December 1959.

Ö. Södergård, "Un aspect de la prose de Camus : le rythme ternaire", *Studia Neophilologica*, Vol. XXXI, 1959.

A. Sonnenfeld, "Albert Camus as Dramatist : The Sources of His Failure", *Tulane Drama Review*, Vol. V, No. 4, June 1961.

H. R. Stockwell, "Albert Camus", *The Cambridge Journal*, Vol. VII, No. 11, 1954.

G. Stourzh, "The Unforgivable Sin : An Interpretation of *The Fall*", *Chicago Review*, Vol. XV, No. 1, Summer 1961.

R. Theis, "Albert Camus' Rückkehr zu Sisyphus", *Romanische Forschungen*, Vol. LXX, 1958.

P. Thody, "Albert Camus", *The Contemporary Review*, Vol. CLXXX, No. 1092, 1956.

S. Ullmann, "The Two Styles of Camus", in : *The Image in the Modern French Novel*, London, 1960.

C. Vigée, "La Nostalgie du sacré chez Albert Camus", *La Nouvelle Revue Française*, No. 87, 1960.

C. Vigée, "L'Errance entre l'exil et le royaume", *La Table Ronde*, No. 146, 1960.

C. A. VIGGIANI, "Camus' *L'Étranger*", P.M.L.A. of America, Vol. LXXI, 1956.

C. A. VIGGIANI, "Albert Camus' First Publications", *Modern Language Notes*, Vol. LXXV, 1960.

Angus WILSON, "Albert Camus, Humanist", *The Spectator*, 26th February 1960.

R. WOLLHEIM, "The Political Philosophy of Existentialism", *Cambridge Journal*, October 1953.

·J.   SOME SPECIAL CAMUS NUMBERS OF CRITICAL JOURNALS ETC.

La Table Ronde, February 1960.

La Nouvelle Revue Française, March 1960.

Preuves, April 1960.

La Revue d'Histoire du Théâtre, October-December 1960.

L'Esprit, January 1960.

Albert Camus, Configuration Critique, Revue des Lettre Modernes, Paris 1961.

À Albert Camus, ses amis du Livre, Gallimard, 1962.

Hommage à Albert Camus des écrivains arabes—Revue du Caire, May 1960.